ONE LAST CAST

ONE
LAST CAST

REFLECTIONS OF
AN OUTDOOR LIFE

BY BRUCE MASTERMAN

RMB

RMB | Rocky Mountain Books Ltd.
rmbooks.com
@rmbooks
facebook.com/rmbooks

Cataloguing data available from Library and Archives Canada
ISBN 978-1-77160-214-3 (paperback)
ISBN 978-1-77160-215-0 (electronic)

Design: Chyla Cardinal

Printed and bound in Canada by Friesens

Distributed in Canada by Heritage Group Distribution and in the U.S. by Publishers Group West

For information on purchasing bulk quantities of this book, or to obtain media excerpts or invite the author to speak at an event, please visit rmbooks.com and select the "Contact Us" tab.

RMB | Rocky Mountain Books is dedicated to the environment and committed to reducing the destruction of old-growth forests. Our books are produced with respect for the future and consideration for the past.

We acknowledge the financial support of the Government of Canada through the Canada Book Fund and the Canada Council for the Arts, and of the province of British Columbia through the British Columbia Arts Council and the Book Publishing Tax Credit.

Canada Council Conseil des arts
for the Arts   du Canada

BRITISH COLUMBIA
ARTS COUNCIL
An agency of the Province of British Columbia

CONTENTS

INTRODUCTION

This book was a long time in the making. In fact, when I wrote most of the pieces you'll find here, I wasn't thinking that one day they would be part of a book.

That all changed a few years back when I started reflecting about the millions of words and thousands of stories I've written so far in my 40-plus-year career as a journalist and non-fiction writer. I decided there was a very clear theme, and together they would make a compelling piece of work. I hope you agree.

The stories in this book mean a great deal to me. I believe they are as relevant today as when they were first written.

Of the 36 stories in this book, the majority have previously appeared in a daily newspaper (the *Calgary Herald*, where I worked as a reporter/columnist for 21 years), international, national or regional magazines, or as chapters in one of the several books to which I've contributed over the years. Four stories have never been published.

The title story, "One Last Cast," has now appeared in print – in one form or another – a total of four times. It originally appeared in the *Calgary Herald* on Sept. 6, 1999. It was published the same day that our eldest daughter, Chelsea, left home to go to university in Lethbridge. At the time I wrote a weekly outdoors column. I decided this was a timely topic. Chelsea gave me her okay to publish it (and the *Herald* graciously allowed it to be reprinted in this book).

The original, the *Herald* version, was written in third person rather than first person. I thought that approach would make it more relevant to all readers because they could identify more clearly with the main characters, Chelsea and me. I wanted it to resonate with every parent reader who has ever had a child leave home and for all the children too. It's a rite of passage that some parents find traumatic. My wife, Karen, and I certainly did.

I received dozens of incredibly touching emails, cards and telephone calls from readers after the column was published. Many said it made them cry. A few said they hugged or called their kids after reading it. I've never had so much reaction to a piece of writing.

That column was the basis of a version that later appeared in both *Reader's Digest* magazine and in the book *Chicken Soup for the Nature Lover's Soul*. The editors of both publications insisted I write it in first person, making it clear that it was about our family. I resisted that approach because I thought it watered it down. But I finally relented. I've always preferred the third-person version for this story, which is why that's what appears in this book.

I consider myself blessed to have been able to focus so much of my career to date on the outdoors, nature and various activities that have taken me to wild places. The outdoors is a lifelong passion, not just a hobby. I live and breathe it, and it helps keep me mentally level, as you'll read in the soul-baring never-before-published story "Into the Light."

This book's subtitle indicates that these are my personal reflections of the outdoors. Although they are, many of the stories focus on other people and their experiences. Some of the stories are meant to inspire and some might make you chuckle. You might not agree with everything you read, and that's okay. It is my hope, however, that these stories might spark a memory of your own, prompt you to think about an event, an emotion or place that means as much to you as the subjects in this book mean to me. Sense of place plays a major role in all these stories.

This is not a *how-to* book. I like to think of it as more of a *why-to* book. It's not about how to be a better hiker, conservationist, naturalist, hunter or angler. It's about why these groups of recreationalists do what they do and why the outdoors is so important to so many lives.

Hopefully you might gain a clearer appreciation and understanding for wild places along with the critters and people that rely on them to live.

One can't spend as much time in the outdoors as I do without the support of family and a great network of friends. I have that, in spades.

My wife, Karen, and daughters, Chelsea and Sarah, are

always supportive of my activities, and my beliefs. They share my passion for nature and for most of the activities described here. The one exception is hunting – they don't hunt but they aren't against it and they all enjoy eating wild game. I try to keep the freezer stocked with venison and game birds.

Fortunately, for me, all three have always been very supportive of the notion that they might be mentioned in my writing. You will see several references to them in this book.

I've also been extremely blessed to be able to share outdoor experiences with my late parents, Marybelle and Bob – Mum far too briefly and Dad into his 80s – stepmother, Margaret; my siblings, Sue, Barb and Rick; along with many other relatives.

Ditto for friends and mentors, who are far too many to name here. These people have shown me the way, allowed me to show them a thing or two, and have shared their stories so that I can tell them to you. Many, but not all, appear in the following pages, sometimes by name and often only by circumstance. Others will make their appearances in future writings.

Any writing is nothing but a private collection of words unless it has readers to read it, to question it and to share the experiences described. I am grateful for the people who have read my writing in newspapers, magazines and books, including this one.

You have given me a great gift. Thank you.

And without the many editors and publishers with whom

I've worked – which now includes Don Gorman of Rocky Mountain Books – my writing would not have had a home and I would have been forced to get a real job that kept me in an office all day. Their support is greatly appreciated.

As a parent and former leader of Junior Forest Wardens and a church youth group, I strongly support the notion that children should be exposed to the outdoors at a young age. It's not only good for them, it's good for the adults they go with. It also helps create a new generation of conservation-minded people who will grow up wanting to ensure wild things and wild places have a secure future.

The book is divided into sections: Seasons, Nature, Kinship, In the Field, On the Water and Connecting the Dots. Seasons describes observations during the four seasons in the year of a marsh. Nature offers a myriad of outdoor tales. Kinship focuses on family and friends. In the Field relates to hunting experiences and On the Water is about fishing. Connecting the Dots traces the highlights of my own journey in the outdoors.

Some might find it surprising to learn that I've always found it rather daunting to write myself into my stories. I'm sometimes afraid to open that Pandora's box because of what might escape for the world to see. I'd rather write about others. It's easier, for one. Less stressful too.

But it is also true that writing about personal experiences is therapeutic. A newspaper colleague liked to say that writing a regular column means never needing a psychiatrist, because your word processing computer is like a therapist's couch, and your readers the therapist.

I find it helpful to share my own experiences in my writing because it forces me to really think about what they meant to me, to help me figure out my place, to determine if they might be relevant to others, and to show the lessons each experience offers.

Alaska author Lynn Schooler talked about this idea in his wonderful book *The Blue Bear*, about his quest for a blue, or glacier, bear and his friendship with a Japanese wildlife photographer who was killed by a grizzly in Russia.

Schooler wrote:

> I never perceived how each and every event and encounter of an entire lifetime, no matter how enormous or small, leads from one to another … in a process as exact as a watchmaker's mind or the return of the salmon, that we might learn those lessons which show us our worth and our place at each moment, until this, the final moment when it is time to write.

I knew when it was time to write the stories on the following pages, and when it was time to compile them into one book.

I hope you enjoy the journey.

Bruce Masterman

SEASONS

SPRING

The transformation verges on the magical. One day, the marsh is frozen and quiet. Just a few days later, it seems, the ice is almost gone and the place is abuzz with wondrous sights and sounds of spring.

Paired off for mating, the first of the returning Canada geese jealously and loudly protect their turf, furiously hissing and charging after all interlopers, regardless of whether they pose a genuine threat. Even muskrats with rapidly wiggling hairless tails must hurry to escape.

Redheads, northern pintails, teal and ruddy ducks paddle furtively among the cattails, watching warily above them for the northern harrier they know is skimming just over the tops of the vegetation, ready to suddenly dive for its dinner. Out on the uplands, wary mallards waddle through the high grasses as they check out potential nest sites safe from enemies wild and not.

Hundreds of Franklin's gulls and their larger cousins, the California gull, cry raucously while circling above the water. From far away comes the sound of more approaching Canada geese, excitedly har-onking their imminent arrival to their brethren already on the water. A bald eagle watches from its perch on a skeletal shoreline poplar. Piercing yellow eyes scan the action, hopefully searching for a faltering wing beat or other weakness that might signal an easy meal.

Compared to the icy tomb of winter, the marsh in early spring is a busy place indeed. And it becomes even busier as the longer days warm the water and vegetation grows green and lush. Before that has a chance to happen, Mother Nature has a tendency to play a cruel joke on her creatures by blanketing the marsh in a late snowfall.

The gulls vanish, flying off to friendlier climes until the snow melts. Geese and ducks bravely hang tough, seemingly accepting the hardship and instinctively knowing that one day the snow and cold will be gone for good. Soon, their eggs hatch and downy peeping puffballs emerge into a strange new world of life and – for many – death.

As the spring drama continues, red-winged and yellow-headed blackbirds arrive to sing and flit about in the cattails. Then grebes face off in showy courtship dances. Finally it is late spring and shorebirds – curlew, godwit, snipe, avocet and sandpiper – take the stage, haunting the shallows in search of plants and insects.

Springtime is not Belle's favourite season in the marsh. During late summer, autumn and winter, our Lab-retriever cross runs free – just a whistle away – as she sniffs coyote scat, flushes pheasants and futilely chases the odd white-tailed jackrabbit. When the water's open, Belle is in it more than she's out.

But from April to August, when there's so much for a dog

to see and do, she is attached to a leash, forced to heel and otherwise stay under tight control. She doesn't like it, but that's the way it has to be.

The springtime marsh is fragile, more so than in any other season. Ironically, it's also a time when more and more people come to visit, to watch birds, take photographs, walk, jog and otherwise shake off winter's emotional and physical mantle. History has shown that increased use can be harmful to any natural environment, especially when it's done irresponsibly.

Accordingly, we treat the marsh differently in spring. We tread more cautiously, stay on established trails, and avoid getting too close to nests or young birds. We don't want to frighten adult birds off nests or risk separating them from their broods, which makes the young easy prey for foxes, gulls, hawks and other predators – including unleashed pet dogs.

What happens in the marsh in spring has a direct bearing on the rest of the year. Human behaviour, weather, habitat and a dozen other factors translate into successful breeding of waterfowl and other wildlife.

Spring on the marsh is more than just a season. It's a feeling – of hope and promise and renewal. It's a time of replenishment for wild species and human spirit.

Belle may not understand that, but we must.

SUMMER

The summer marsh has a certain natural rhythm that is so different from the other three seasons.

Life in summer is unfolding as it should. The many and diverse wetlands creatures go through their daily routines as they were created to do, unhurried and by rote, honing survival skills shaped by evolution and adapted to present times.

The ducks and geese eat, rest, socialize, watch and train their young to survive, and they do this day after long summer day. Young wings get stronger each day, preparing for their first major journey – their destiny. The birds seem content in this rhythm, knowing it will be several weeks before the urge to migrate becomes so undeniably strong that it will be time to take flight for the long trip south.

Except for twice-daily forays to feed in nearby fields, most waterfowl species don't move far from the water on these hot summer days. Along with the shorebirds, they hang close to their broods, warily eyeing a coyote that ventures too close, or a gull that swoops menacingly in search of lunch. They swim around the edges, forming larger and larger flocks as helpless fledglings develop into young adults with an ingrained sense of safety in numbers.

To many, the bird life is the natural pulse of the marsh, the outward sign of life of a body of water fringed in cattails and bulrushes. Some people, it seems, need to see the birds in order to know there is a pulse, to be assured that life exists in this oasis of water and rich grassland on the drought-parched prairie.

Nature knows better. Nature knows the pulse doesn't need to be seen to be there, that it also lies under the surface of the marsh, strong and throbbing and never-ending, like a beating heart.

The pulse is the backswimmers, freshwater shrimp and other tiny aquatic creatures that become visible only if you look hard for them. It is the muskrats that swim among the green grasses, nibbling off succulent stalks and taking them back to their dens, where hungry youngsters await.

The pulse is the mink that darts furtively through the greenery, seldom seen by human visitors but a deadly presence nevertheless. It is the garter snake that slinks through the grass, occasionally slipping into the water and swimming in pronounced S-curves with its head raised like a periscope, extended tongue testing the air like a wolf sniffing out its prey. And the pulse is the crickets and the frogs, regularly heard but seldom seen.

It is in summer that it becomes all too apparent that more than wild creatures depend on the marsh for life or, perhaps more accurately, quality of life.

It is a late July afternoon. The sun is starting to slide down toward the western horizon. Mallards and pintails scoot over the water, and great flocks of Canada geese are heading out to feed. A northern harrier skims low over the tops of the cattails.

Turning to watch the activity around me, I notice movement on an earthen berm several hundred metres away. A middle-aged woman, in shorts and T-shirt, jogs easily along a dirt trail.

My binoculars reveal the woman has a yellow tape player strapped to her waist, a cord running to earphones on her head. Seemingly oblivious to the natural choir of honks and quacks all around her, she is lost in her own world. Although her ears are closed, her eyes are not.

From a sheltered bay close to her, a flock of Canada geese lifts off, noisily. Suddenly 75 of the big birds are in the air a stone's throw from the woman. Her pace slows to a walk. Her head turns and she watches the flock until it disappears over a rise.

As the woman resumes her run, her gait seems stronger and more determined than ever. She occasionally glances at the spot where she last saw the geese, as if she's willing them to return.

Unwittingly, she is caught in the rhythm, and has become a part of the pulse of the summer marsh.

AUTUMN

A heavy curtain of fog enveloped the marsh on this early October morning.

The day had started rather inauspiciously. The drive from town took longer than usual, with the mist making the van's headlights almost useless. I narrowly missed a mule deer doe that suddenly materialized on the gravel road.

Then, after loading the 12-foot rowboat with shotgun, decoys, extra gear and my sometimes-faithful dog, Belle, I stepped into the water to push the craft into deeper water. That's when I discovered the leaky waders I'd vowed to patch – but hadn't – were filling with icy water, chilling my feet to the bone.

After we got underway, I soon realized my navigational skills were somewhat lacking. The fog obscured the distant farm light I usually used as a guiding beacon. Guided only by instinct, I pulled the oars steadily and aimed for the far shore.

Amazingly, over the next hour, with unseen ducks whistling by overhead, I rowed in a complete circle, returning to the parked van. This happened not once, but twice.

Finally, I opted to hug the shoreline while seeking a thick patch of bulrushes a few hundred metres to the east. Several minutes later – and now well into legal shooting time – I stopped at the first promising-looking spot and tossed a dozen mallard decoys and one floating fake Canada goose into a crude S-pattern. Then I backed the boat into the bulrushes and poured tea from the Thermos.

I didn't see the first ducks come in, but Belle did. Her whining alerted me to a trio of mallards just as they vanished into the fog. Belle looked quizzical, as if wondering why I hadn't shot.

Raising the cup of steaming Earl Grey to my mouth, I looked up just as a hen and drake pintail skimmed over the decoys and disappeared. I quickly gulped down most of the tea and picked up the battered old pump gun.

Naturally, the action promptly stopped. Nothing flew for the next 20 minutes, at least not anything we could see. Belle perched on the plywood bow seat and watched intently, cocking her ears at the sound of ducks flying or splashing down beyond our view. The mist defined our world, reducing visibility to an area the size of my backyard.

Suddenly, a distant sound caused my heart to quicken and Belle's tail to thump against the aluminum gunwale. A lone Canada goose was approaching. I strained to glimpse it through the haze but couldn't see a thing. Then, all was silent and I assumed the goose had gone elsewhere.

Just as I reached for my tea, the goose broke through the cloud, set its wings and coasted toward the decoys

25 metres away. I lifted the shotgun and fired. The goose landed with a splash.

Every hunter hopes and strives for a clean, quick kill, the ultimate culmination of this tradition-steeped autumn ritual that only those who do it can ever fully understand.

So when the goose started swimming away trailing a broken wing, I felt my heart sink. In a flash, Belle was in the water after it. The wounded goose quickened its pace and soon vanished in the fog.

Her black body cutting the still grey water, using her tail as a rudder, Belle followed the bird into the gloom. For several long minutes, I saw and heard nothing. Several more ducks flew into the decoys, but I sat motionless, knowing it would be wrong to shoot when my last shot remained unresolved.

I started calling Belle's name, and blew the comeback command on the whistle she almost always obeys. The sounds faded into the mist, just as Belle and the goose had done.

As I prepared to pull anchor and head off in search of her, I was stopped by a slight splash beyond the decoys. Paddling out of the fog like a ghostly vision, Belle churned the water with her front paws as she slowly paddled toward the boat. Breathing hard and sputtering, she was exhausted.

But as I praised her while removing the dead goose from her mouth and helping her in, the fatigue seemed to lift.

A few minutes later, so did the fog. The hunt was over.

We didn't need any more birds on this day. Belle had done her job to perfection, even as I had not.

"Let's go home," I told Belle, rubbing her head.

She didn't argue.

WINTER

The marsh looks barren and lifeless.

Blanketed in snow and ice, it looks so different than just a few short months ago, when the water was alive with migrating waterfowl and murky waves lapped against the shore. The waves have been stilled, transformed into a sheet of ice.

The cattails and bulrushes stand tall and defiant, hoarfrost dusting their stalks. It seems a lifetime ago that I eased a rowboat into those same stalks, tossed out a dozen decoys and waited for magic time.

But that was another day, another season.

Now Belle, whiskers white with frost and black muzzle grizzled with snow, runs atop the same water in which she usually swims. She dashes around in pure doggy joy, stopping only to sniff a muskrat house or some critter's frozen scat.

And, yes, there are critters. Lots of them. The winter marsh may look lifeless, but it's not.

In 1948, Aldo Leopold wrote in *A Sand County Almanac*: "January observation can be almost as simple and peaceful as snow, and almost as continuous as cold. There is time not only to see who has done what, but to speculate why."

In the marsh on this frozen day, I savour the speculation and beauty even as I pull the wool toque down over my ears.

Single-line coyote tracks bisect the snow. Their strategy seems simple – sniff out muskrat dens, wood snags and territorial markings. They've stopped at every clump of grass, hopefully nosing each in search of a meal.

Tiny pairs of mouse paw prints look like giant zippers connecting clumps of bulrushes. One track leads away from the protective cover, heading toward a lone clump 50 yards away. Halfway there, it abruptly stops.

Wing-type indentations in the snow bracket the final set of paw prints. I wonder if the mouse even heard the owl before it struck.

Belle and I continue our journey of discovery and speculation. We leave the ice and head out across the snowy grasslands.

Suddenly, Belle's tail starts wagging like a metronome on speed and she hits overdrive. The ring-necked pheasant rooster cackles madly as it flushes and flies away. I smile. Where were you last fall, I ask aloud, and what are you doing this far from the protection of the bulrushes? Feeling silly, I look around to make sure nobody is listening.

But I know we're alone. The marsh in winter does that to people. Keeps them away in droves, which is good for speculators like me and dogs like Belle. For some reason, there's a common misconception that nothing happens at the marsh in winter. I silently give thanks for this common belief and the privacy it creates.

After crossing the uplands, we return to the ice. I spy some tracks I don't see often. Mink. The paws are little more than an inch wide and less than two long. Each paw has five toes, showing tiny claw marks in the skiff. The tracks meander across the ice, the animal's gait alternating between walking and bounding.

Twice, the trail is swept away by wind, and I search in ever-widening circles before I pick it up again. I follow the prints for a half mile, stopping periodically to peer well ahead with my binoculars, hoping for a glimpse of the animal itself. Eventually, the trail disappears completely and I reluctantly turn away.

We swing north toward the vehicle. Something looks out of place atop a signpost 300 yards ahead. Through binoculars, I see a plump white body with two yellow eyes peering back at me. A snowy owl.

A movement behind it diverts my attention. A bushy-coated coyote wanders out of a patch of cattails, stops and sits down on the ice. Amazingly, I can see both owl and coyote in the same sight picture. It's like watching nature on television.

After a few minutes of watching them watching us, it's time to go. The marsh has given us enough action – and speculation – for one winter day.

NATURE

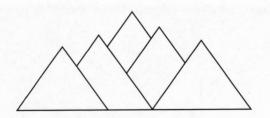

THE BEST SEAT
IN THE HOUSE

It was a long winter. Snow arrived in mid-November and didn't leave until early April, when a day or two of sun and relative warmth erased most of the white stuff from the landscape. We all breathed a collective sigh of relief, thankful spring had finally arrived and we could finally doff our winter clothes and go hiking.

But then, as it tends to do, winter returned with a vengeance. A spring snowstorm blew in, making driving treacherous and forcing us all back to snow shovels and fleece-lined snow boots. Many people grumbled and stayed inside. Others, like us, couldn't have been happier.

My wife, Karen, and I, along with friends Penny and Tony, saw the weather as a blessing, a chance for a bonus late-season snowshoeing outing in the hills. We grabbed our snowshoes, poles and boots, packed lunch and headed west to a little-known provincial park tucked away in the foothills. We knew the fresh deep snow would keep most people at home that day, but we soldiered on, almost giddy with excitement of what lay ahead. Even though we almost got stuck when we pulled into the parking lot, our mood remained bright as we readied our gear and set off on the trail.

Suddenly, we were enveloped in one of those rare winter-wonderland Christmas-card scenes. Soft snow blanketed the ground and shrouded the forest of lodgepole pines, white spruce and poplars. The sun shone down from an azure-blue sky, shooting shafts of light through the trees and onto the virgin snow. The air we hungrily inhaled was fresh and smelled faintly of pine.

It was the kind of place that Scottish-American naturalist John Muir might have been thinking about when he wrote: "Everybody needs beauty as well as bread, places to play in and pray in where nature may heal and cheer and give strength to the body and soul."

We trudged single file along the trail threading the trees. We stopped often, to look at fresh deer or squirrel tracks, or to just bask in the quiet beauty. Later, a deer would scamper across the trail in front of us. Sometimes we had to stop to catch our breath. The trail was climbing and the snow was soft and sticky, making the going tough at times.

Although challenged by the physical exertion, we were guided by Muir's words. We all drew strength from our environment, allowing the serenity of the place to infuse our souls and refresh our bodies. We soon gained the top of the ridge, where we were greeted by a spectacular expansive view of foothills rolling like giant waves out to the snow-covered Rocky Mountains. We sat on a bench, eating our lunches of fruit, crackers and red licorice washed down with chai tea and water.

"Well, this sure beats staying home complaining about the snow," somebody said. Everyone nodded.

That's one great thing about the outdoors. If we open ourselves to all that the outdoors has to offer, we open ourselves to be blessed with experiences such as this one. I call them bonus trips. They happen only if we make them happen, if we not only recognize an opportunity but seize it.

Outdoors enthusiasts are resilient, opportunistic people. We tend to respond positively to factors and situations that could be perceived as negatives – a late-season snowfall, for example.

I thought of that a few weeks ago while we drove through the state of Washington, en route to San Francisco. It was a glorious, sunny day and the drive was pleasant. But the wind was blasting with such ferocity that it had turned the Columbia River Gorge into a wind tunnel. High, crashing whitecaps churned the river's surface into an angry froth.

The occasional barge plied the river, but all smaller craft were safely still at dock. The Columbia is famous for fishing, but the anglers stayed home this day. The only sign of life was a few gulls playing in the wind.

Suddenly, Karen spotted what she thought was a white pelican soaring in the wind. Seconds later, she corrected herself. "It's a kite," she said, "with somebody flying along below it."

Sure enough, when we stopped the vehicle we saw wet-suit-clad people sailing on surfboards. One was tethered to a giant kite as he skipped over the waves, occasionally allowing the wind to lift and carry him aloft for several yards before touching down again. Two others were on sailboards – basically surfboards equipped with a main sail – holding on tight as they turned and twisted in the waves.

They were all using the power of the wind to enjoy the ride of their lives.

Several miles down the highway, we came across a similar scene, but with more than a dozen sailboarders and kite surfers on the water at any one time. Dozens of people sat on lawn chairs, watching the action and perhaps waiting their turn.

Standing on the shoreline, I was buffeted by the relentless wind. A smaller person would have been in danger of flying away. Even though the camera was affixed to a sturdy tripod, I struggled to keep it steady.

A young man, carrying a sailboard, walked by me, heading for the wild water. He looked over with a smile as wide as the gorge itself and said, "You've got the best seat in the house."

He was right. It *was* the best seat in the house. Then again, it's always the best seat in the house if you let it be.

STAIRWAY TO HEAVEN

The ridge has called my name for more than 30 years.

It looms high above the scenic river valley in the Rocky Mountains west of the foothills town where we live. It's a steep, west-facing slope, which means it loses snow early in the spring, and most years is carpeted by May in a soft blanket of lush green grass and wildflowers.

I've cycled the paved highway that winds its way north along the valley, and I've caught trout in the river that flows adjacent to the road. Whenever I've played at the base of the ridge I've found myself peering longingly high above me and wondered what it would be like to be way up there.

I always wondered whether I'd be able to do it, physically, or whether my bum hip and knee would force me to turn around partway up. Nobody likes having to turn around.

Someday, I kept thinking, I will find out. But that day never came. Year after year passed and I still hadn't climbed the ridge. Friends would regale me with tales of having done it. They'd breathlessly describe it as if it were a spiritual experience.

My response would be mixed; although happy for them, I was upset at myself for not making it happen, year after year after year. It seems I always had an excuse – too sore, too fat, too old, too busy.

On May 7, after a winter of physical sloth and a frenetic work and volunteer schedule, I was sitting in my office, watching doves and robins splash in the bird bath as I contemplated death. Not my own, but those of two close friends within a week.

Both were younger than 70, and both had gone quickly. I didn't have a chance to say goodbye to one of them, and the other didn't know I was even there when I visited the afternoon before he passed. As I sat pondering mortality, inspiration struck. Today I would hike the ridge.

I quickly pack a water bottle, lunch, bear spray, binoculars and hiking poles. Less than an hour later, I stand beside the car and ponder the ridge looming high above me. I note its steepness, as if seeing for the first time how very far it is to the top. It is an ambitious first hike of the season, to be sure, but it's time. Past time.

The day is warm and sunny with a strong west wind. The first few hundred yards go well, even though I can't seem to catch my breath. I've been fighting a cold, and the extra pounds aren't helping. I stop often to take pictures and savour the view of snow-covered mountains and the river flowing peacefully far below. Brilliant mauve prairie crocuses punctuate the landscape.

I reach the edge of a poplar grove. A flicker of white in the trees gives away three whitetail deer, grazing peacefully just 70 yards away. I silently sneak away to leave them in peace.

I'm serenaded by a constant chorus of Columbian ground squirrels, their voices sharp, high-pitched squeaks. Some run for cover in their dens but many do not. They watch, curious yet undisturbed, as I walk past. At the start of the hike, several golden eagles circled in the thermals above me; as I climb higher, some fly below me

An hour later, just about two-thirds of the way to the top, I'm breathing heavily and my winter-weary muscles are complaining. I sit on a flat boulder, where I sip water and eat orange slices and barbecued elk steak left over from supper the night before. The elk is courtesy of my friend Tom, who was pushing 80 last November when he shot a fat cow near his log cabin, not 20 yards from where I tagged a whitetail buck just a few days earlier.

Evidence of elk surrounds me. The ground is indented with hoofprints and covered with droppings. I stop often to glass the openings on the ridge, hoping to see an elk. I'm also eager to see a black or grizzly bear, but preferably not on the ridge that I'm on.

I continue my slog upward; the top of the ridge is 75 yards away. But when I get there, it proves to be a false summit, as there's yet another hill beyond it. A few minutes later, I top out. I finally made it. I can't stop smiling.

Here, the elk droppings are fresher – moist and soft when I poke them with a hiking pole. Suddenly, I smell elk. Their odour is heavy, musky, and I know they are close. I advance cautiously, using spruce and poplars for cover.

Then, there they are: four cow elk standing in a clearing a stone's throw away. Although the wind is in my favour and I've tried to be stealthy, they've made me. Their tawny bodies are on full alert, ears upright as they peer directly at me.

On silent cue, they begin trotting, then disappear over a hill. I explore the ridge top for an hour – spying several more elk, one feeding just 50 yards away – before I find a thick fallen log to sit on. For 30 minutes, I use the binoculars to scan the surrounding mountains, ridges and clearings, and the river far below.

There are elk everywhere, small herds of feeding cows and yearlings. The bulls have lost their ivory-tipped antlers, but I spy a few small bachelor herds and one big old buckskin-coloured boy on a distant ridge. I also spot small bunches of mule deer and three more whitetails.

From my high vantage point, I inhale the clear spring air and marvel at the view. I silently give thanks for the experience, the strength to get here and for good friends and family, past and present. I have finally made it to the top of the ridge. It took me 90 minutes of actual hiking, but the journey began more than three decades ago.

And now that I'm here I don't want to leave.

INTO THE LIGHT

A few years ago, I was in the sitting-room of a Victorian-style house, talking with a group of women struggling with addictions and various mental health issues, including depression. Ranging in age from teens to middle-aged, they had voluntarily enrolled in a recovery program called Narrow Road Home. Soon our conversation turned to depression, commonly considered either a root cause or result of dependencies on drugs and alcohol. When I mentioned my own journey with depression, some in the room expressed surprise.

"But you seem so cheery," one said, smiling.

Another woman asked how I dealt with depression.

"I self-medicate," I replied, evoking a few uneasy glances around the room.

Then I quickly added, "I prescribe myself generous regular doses of the outdoors whenever I'm feeling down. Being in nature helps level out my emotional peaks and valleys."

My response may have seemed rather simplistic, especially considering these women were facing the toughest fight of their lives, but it is true. When I become mired in depression, or feel the early symptoms of its onset, I head outdoors for a hike or snowshoe, or to fly-fish or hunt, or just to seek quiet sanctuary in a marsh, a peaceful hillside, a mountain trail. Whether it's for an hour or a day, I always go home feeling better, more energized, more hopeful. Being outdoors is my personal pathway from darkness into the light.

"Nature ... cheaper than therapy," reads a small wooden sign that sits on a book shelf near my desk. Some people might consider the sentiment it expresses as being flippant. Not to me. It's my mantra, a constant reminder of my chosen way of handling depression, the most common form of mental illness.

I recall that depression became a part of my life when I was a teenager. Although depression isn't always caused by a major life event, I've always linked mine with the death of my mother to cancer when she was 46 and I was 15. It was a traumatic life-changing event for my three siblings and our father. We all responded in different ways. I became moody and withdrawn, angry at the world. Depressed.

Depression and *depressed* go by other names, including melancholy, morose, down-hearted, blue funk and downcast. The most appropriate, at least for me, is Black Dog. The name was popularized by Winston Churchill to describe his own depression and later used as a title of a book about the condition. In those early days, I learned that depression is relentless. Metaphorically, it goes from constantly tugging at the leash to breaking free, wreaking havoc on our lives and on those around us.

Happily, though, through my 20s and 30s, for some reason the Black Dog took a nap. My depression all but vanished. I went to college, started a career in journalism, married a wonderful woman, and we had two fabulous daughters. We lived in a comfortable house in a beautiful little town. I had a daily newspaper reporting job envied by many. Much of my time was spent writing about conservation and the environment, interests which were and are dear to my heart.

And then, inexplicably, the Black Dog awoke. My nemesis slowly started to worm its way back into my life. At a time when I should have felt on top of the world, I was back riding an emotional roller coaster I felt powerless to control. Many days I was wracked with severe self-doubt and felt worthless despite the best efforts of friends and family to raise me up. I became a master of deception, acting like life was grand, joking around, and generally carrying on as best as I could in my roles as father, husband, brother, friend, community volunteer and newspaper reporter. During this time I tried various medications prescribed by my doctor, but they either had no effect or made me feel worse.

It was during this challenging period that I made a joyful discovery: being outdoors, experiencing nature with all my senses, made me feel better both mentally and physically. Being there not just in body but also in heart and soul.

Feeling the soil beneath my feet and the water as I waded enveloping my body. Closing my eyes and inhaling the cool morning air. Seeing little girls build fairy villages out of stones, sticks and flowers. Basking in the moonlight. Feeling the rough bark of a cottonwood and the sticky sap of a pine tree. Smelling wet leaves after a rain, the fragrance of wildflowers or the muskiness of elk. Hearing the trickle of a clear spring or the call of black-capped chickadee. Revelling in nature's varied colourful palette. Watching a deer slipping through the trees, a trout rising to sip an insect from the surface or the moon reflecting on still water. Giving thanks to God for it all and for the strength to experience it.

Once I learned to experience nature in its multi-faceted fullness, experiencing it as it should be experienced, heading out with my family, solo or with friends became a magic elixir that helped keep the emotional beast at heel. That's when I decided that self-medicating with generous and regular doses of outdoor experiences would be my lifelong plan.

Anne Frank, German-born writer and Holocaust victim, was much younger than I was when she recognized and so eloquently described the benefits of being outdoors. She wrote:

> The best remedy for those who are afraid,
> lonely, or unhappy is to go outside, somewhere
> where they can be quite alone with the heavens,
> nature and God. Because only then does one feel
> that all is as it should be and that God wishes
> to see people happy amidst the simple beauty

of nature … I firmly believe that nature brings
solace in all troubles.

Several decades after Frank's death in a concentration camp, the Internet brims with information linking nature experiences with mental health. One authority to whom I was drawn is Leslie Davenport, author of the classic book *Healing and Transformation Through Self-Guided Imagery*. A founding member of the Institute for Health and Healing at California Pacific Medical Center in San Francisco, Davenport is a pioneer in the health care revolution that recognizes psycho-spiritual dimensions as an integral part of health.

Davenport says that it should come as no surprise that as alienation from nature increases, so does depression. With mental health disorders expected to rise to 15 per cent of the global burden of disease by the year 2020, Davenport notes that depression alone constitutes one of the largest health problems worldwide. With more than half the world's population living in cities, she points out, many people go through the day with little or no contact with the natural environment.

Poetically, we could say that being in nature
wakes up our ancestral roots, those instincts
tuned to the earth rhythms of the seasons. Some
part of us recognizes that the ecosystem is the
essential currency in which all life depends. Or

47

perhaps when we witness the roots of the trees growing into the stream and the leaves tipping upward to be nurtured by the sun, it's just easier to register the way life self-organizes into a functional, interdependent whole.

Davenport correctly notes that people are really good at being somewhere other than where we are. We dream of being home while at our work desks, create our shopping list while driving and worry about our career over the weekend. The key, she says, is to shift out of our thinking mind and into our senses. When you're in nature, Davenport says, "Let the time be yours to rest, walk or explore. If your thoughts wander back to habitual worries or planning, remember you can always renew the choice to come to your senses. And research tells us you'll be happy you did."

Depression comes in various forms and seldom signals when it's going to strike. When it does, it affects its victims at varying levels of severity. There is no simple, one-size-fits-all answer as to how to try to live with it. It might be medication, or counselling, or a combination of the two, perhaps along with exercise or heightened involvement in an activity that ignites your passion.

For me, coming to my senses – all my senses – while in the outdoors is key to my physical, mental and spiritual health.

It's a place where my own Black Dog never goes off-leash.

THE NOT-SO-SECRET
PLACE

I call it "my secret cutthroat lake" but there's really nothing too secret about it.

After all, this remote destination is listed in various fishing and hiking guidebooks, and appears on most maps. A local university's outdoor program centre even conducts guided hikes into the lake hugging the Alberta–British Columbia border.

Although it may be far from secret, I still consider the Lake That Shall Not Be Named my own private refuge, a special place where yours truly and whoever I'm with are often the only people there.

Many of us who spend time in the outdoors have places we consider special. They are life-giving places that soothe our souls with their beauty and an atmosphere that would create instant millionaires if it could be canned and sold.

This not-so-hidden jewel in the Rocky Mountains is mine.

The lake isn't big; it's split into two basins that would fit into two football fields. But it is nestled in a mind-blowing setting. It's bracketed at the far end with a rocky headwall, which drops down into an avalanche slope of fallen rock and dead trees. Turn slightly and you'll see a vista of lush green mountain meadows. Turn completely around and there's a mountain that's snow-capped year-round. On the other side is a boggy willow patch leading to a forest of spruce and pine trees.

The silence there is usually broken only by the occasional squeaks of pikas – soft-furred creatures some call rock rabbits – and Columbian ground squirrels.

When I was there last week, we were blessed with another sound: the piercing cry of an osprey flying overhead. It was eyeing the fat west-slope cutthroat trout that cruise the clear, blue, usually glass-calm water, enticing to fishers both legged and winged.

Some outdoors enthusiasts like keeping their special places to themselves. Although I feel that way about some places, for some strange reason I love sharing this one with people who I know will appreciate it.

Many years ago, I hiked in with a magazine editor visiting from Manitoba, a province not exactly known for its mountain landscapes. (Yes, I know; Riding Mountain National Park and the Turtle Mountains are indeed beautiful, but they are mountains in name more than geological formation).

When I first told her about this special place, she asked if there were any bears. The question is valid; grizzly and black bears live in this area, with more of the former than the latter.

I've seen grizzly tracks in the mud on the trail, and the terrain surrounding the lake is often gouged with so many fresh bear diggings that it looks like a backhoe has been at work. One afternoon last summer, four days after I was there with my wife and her family visiting from Manitoba, a big grizzly ambled along the shoreline while several fly-fishers cast in the water. "I could have hit it with my back cast," one of them excitedly told me the next day.

Several years ago, I arrived at the trailhead with two fly-fishers from the city, who had bought the trip I'd donated to a fundraising silent auction. On the drive to the trailhead, they'd talked anxiously about the prospect of a bear encounter. No sooner had we parked the vehicle and started removing gear from the back of the vehicle than a grizzly strolled out of the trees 50 metres away. After I pointed it out, the anglers' eyes became wide as pie plates, and they started jabbering about leaving and fishing elsewhere.

I shushed them and said we'd wait to see what the bear decided for us. The grizzly crossed the road toward us and then ambled north along the highway, away from the trailhead, before finally disappearing in the trees. After I casually checked to ensure my canister of pepper spray was in a holster strapped to my backpack, we hiked in and enjoyed a wonderful trout-filled – and bear-free – day at "my" lake.

I thought of that bear the day I visited with my friend the magazine editor. "My husband is really worried I'll get eaten by a bear, and frankly so am I," she said. I assured her that if we were vigilant and made lots of noise on the hike in, we'd be just fine.

Besides, I said, it would be neat to see a bear – especially a grizzly – at a safe distance. Since grizzlies don't live in Manitoba, I suggested, seeing one in Alberta would add icing to an already sweet experience. She wasn't convinced.

As it turned out that hot and sunny summer day, we didn't see a bear, or even any evidence of one, which made her happy and me a little less so.

But my friend's initial reaction to the place where grizzlies live was epic. As we broke out of the trees and saw the lake surface shimmering like a zillion diamonds against a stunning vista the world's best landscape artist could never adequately capture, she suddenly stopped walking.

As she gazed around in wide-eyed wonder, tears started streaming down her face.

"What's wrong?" I asked, afraid she'd turned an ankle on the hike in.

"Nothing is wrong," she replied. "It's just that I've never been in such a beautiful place."

Just about everyone I share this special place with feels the same way the first time they experience it.

It's how I feel each and every time I visit – with or without the grizzlies.

BIRD IN THE HAND

It was a clear November morning, with the temperature pushing minus-30. The snow lay deep in the fields and woods of west-central Alberta, where my friend Jim and I had just spent a few chilly hours unsuccessfully hunting elusive deer. We were returning to his log house beside the Clearwater River when Jim suddenly told me to stop the vehicle. "There's something out in that field," he said.

Even with binoculars, we couldn't identify the dark, frost-coated creature lying in the snow just ten paces from the road. Then it raised its black face and peered our way with blood-red eyes. Jim and I exchanged incredulous looks. We instantly recognized it as a western grebe, a water bird that should have left Alberta for warmer climes along the Pacific coast at least a month earlier. It certainly shouldn't have been sitting in a snow-covered field two kilometres from the nearest open water.

Left where it was, the bird faced certain death. Grebes can't take off from land, let alone snow. They need to run on top of water to get up enough speed to take flight. Clearly, this particular bird needed help if it was going to survive.

It didn't move or make a sound as we approached. Marks in the surrounding snow, made by talons and broad wings, told of an overnight drama – I imagined the grebe's darting, stiletto-like yellow bill fending off a hungry great horned owl or a determined bald eagle. Jim gently placed his blaze-orange coat over the bird and carefully cradled it in his arms, and we raced back to the van.

After unwrapping the grebe at Jim's house, we immediately saw the reason for its dilemma: it was entangled in two feet of heavy monofilament fishing line, and attached to the line was a large hook, firmly imbedded in the grebe's downy breast. No wonder it couldn't fly.

The bird seemed unusually calm in Jim's hands as I disentangled it from the fishing line and removed the hook. And when we lay it on the snowy driveway, it immediately relaxed and started preening itself in the sunlight, appearing none the worse for wear.

Jim and I marvelled at the bird's plumage as we talked of the challenges facing wild creatures, some natural and others not at all, like the hook and line. Above all, though, we were in awe of the grebe's calm courage after such a harrowing ordeal, and its obvious determination to overcome its man-made handicap – and survive.

Minutes later, Jim picked up the bird and we walked down to the river. It was already frozen along the edges, and many chunks of ice were flowing downstream. When Jim carefully placed the grebe on the icy shoreline, it scuttled the few feet to open water and jumped in. As soon as it started swimming, it dove time and time again, seemingly revelling in its freedom. If a bird could show happiness, this one was definitely ecstatic.

Have you ever noticed that the some of the sweetest experiences afield have nothing to do with the actual hunt, fishing trip or hike? This was one of them. Oh sure, it's a great feeling to top out on a ridge with a spectacular panoramic mountain view after a heart-testing hike, or hook a bruiser brown trout on a tiny dry fly, or bear down on a flock of emerald-headed mallards dropping into your decoys.

But often it's the unrelated things that provide those special memories that stay with us, improving with age. That notion has struck me many times in my 40-plus years afield, but never as poignantly as it did last November as Jim and I watched quietly until the grebe eventually disappeared around the bend in the river.

Thanks to our chance encounter, it could finally begin its journey south.

THE SURVIVOR

The Rocky Mountains in southwestern Alberta watch over a remote, unpopulated chunk of wild land with a near-mystical, siren-like attraction to a certain breed of outdoor enthusiast. For here you can go all day without seeing another person, set up your tent wherever you please, follow game trails unmarked by human signs and fish places visited by few.

Ray Walker was one of those enthusiasts. It was more than 20 years ago now that he was first drawn to the ridges, the wildness and the trout that inhabit the region's high mountain lakes and clear streams. He spent countless hours alone on the old logging roads and ridgelines, seeking those hidden gems of water that held native westslope cutthroat trout as well as introduced golden trout.

The trout were certainly among the rewards for his hours of pushing his trim, five-foot-ten-inch, 160-pound frame up the scree-covered avalanche slopes and steep ridges. And the names of the lakes he fished reflected the area's nature: North Fork, Rainy Ridge, Grizzly.

"Fishing was just one reason I was there," he says, adding he also dreamed of one day running into a living legend whom he'd long admired, the late Andy Russell. The famous author and outdoorsman grew up nearby and regularly hiked and rode horseback over the same vast region bordering the Alberta–BC border northwest of Waterton Lakes National Park.

In fact, the area became the setting for many of Russell's books, including *Grizzly Country*, in which he displayed an admiration for grizzlies leavened with caution. "There are a thousand ways to get into trouble in the mountains," he wrote, "but few of them are as dramatic or as spectacular as a nose-to-nose confrontation with a grizzly."

Although Walker never did meet Russell, those words came glaringly, painfully true one day in 1998. That's when Walker unwittingly encountered a grizzly sow with two cubs, provoking a bloody attack. His life didn't end that day, but what happened to him you wouldn't wish upon your worst enemy.

July 13, 1998, was warm and sunny. Walker, then a 65-year-old retired widower recovering from open-heart surgery, was hiking back to his van after four days of backcountry rambling. While walking through some thick alders, he sang loudly as a precaution against bears. Then the trail opened up, and he stopped singing.

Approaching a creek lined with alders, Walker spotted a dark-brown grizzly about 50 feet away. Almost instantly, a half-grown cub appeared beside her, followed by a second cub emerging from the alders, standing on its hind legs to see him better. "I didn't have time to think at all," he calmly recalls many years later while sitting in the kitchen of his Calgary bachelor apartment. "But I knew I was in trouble when I saw the cubs."

The sow turned briefly, as if to walk away, but in a flash, turned back and came for Walker, soundlessly covering the distance between them in three great bounds. Walker was still standing when the bear swiped a massive, scimitar-clawed front paw at his head. The blow removed his left eye, nose and half his right eyelid. Knocked unconscious, he landed face down.

He awoke to the bear biting the top of his head, and when he interlocked his hands to protect the back of his neck, the bear bit through a finger. Walker willed himself to remain silent and motionless, hoping the grizzly would realize he was no longer a threat. It worked. A few seconds later, the biting stopped and he sensed the bear was gone.

When Walker tentatively raised his head to look around, the sow was nowhere to be seen. He immediately knew what he had to do. "My only thought was to get out of there while I was alive." Standing, he soon realized he could no longer see properly. He dabbed his remaining eye with a tissue, clearing the streaming blood until he could see enough to differentiate between trail and trees.

Having not come across another soul all day, Walker knew he had to save himself. He immediately started walking the remaining three kilometres back to his parked van, stopping often to wipe blood away so he could see. After what seemed a lifetime, he reached his van and somehow managed to drive 30 kilometres over rough, dirt logging roads, gravel roads and finally paved highway to a store in the village of Beaver Mines. "This man must have had a will of iron to make it out from where he was," a local RCMP officer was later quoted as saying. "He's one tough cookie."

From the store, a customer drove Walker to meet an ambulance speeding from Pincher Creek. Then a small plane rushed him to Foothills Hospital in Calgary, 200 kilometres to the north. Despite all this frantic activity and despite the pain, what stands out most in Walker's memory is something he told an RCMP officer: "Whatever happens to me, please don't let that bear be killed. She was only protecting her cubs."

As it turned out, provincial Fish and Wildlife officers closed the area for several days, but they agreed the sow should not be destroyed, because it had been a defensive attack, not a predatory one. Such is not always the case.

Four weeks later, as Walker recovered in a Calgary hospital, another southern Alberta angler, Christopher Kress, was mauled to death by a male grizzly while he fished in the South Castle River, not far from Beaver Mines. Government records show the attack started on the riverbank and ended in the middle of the river. The man's friends, camping nearby, shot and killed the 200-pound bruin. Investigators concluded it had deliberately targeted the anglers as prey – a rarer type of attack.

Lying in his hospital bed for seven long, heavily medicated weeks, Walker had plenty of time to relive his ordeal, and to try to figure out how things went so horribly wrong that day. He realizes he should have been making more noise as he hiked. He also thinks the bear wouldn't have done as much damage if he'd fallen to the ground before she hit him. Although using pepper spray likely would have deterred the bear, Walker doubts he would have had time to unholster it.

Walker endured three major operations. Doctors removed skin from his left forearm and bone from his forehead, using it to rebuild his nose and repair the heavily damaged left side of his face and nose. For a while, whenever he touched his nose, it felt like he was touching his forehead. The grafted skin, as it set, had a lighter complexion than the rest of his face. It still does. Although doctors couldn't do anything about his missing left eye, they managed to sew up his right eyelid. By the time it was all over, Walker had lost more than 25 pounds off his already wiry frame.

The 76-year-old still shows the attack's physical scars. In stores, people stare at his disfigured face, and sometimes children screw up the courage to ask him what happened. He tells them he was in an accident. If he recounted the whole story, he believes, they would grow up with an unreasonable fear of bears, instead of a healthy respect.

While recuperating, Walker kept thinking about how he could put a positive spin on the attack. The only thing he could come up with was that he needed to help educate people about staying safe in bear country. He has since published articles, spoken to outdoors groups and schools, and appeared in bear safety videos – all in the hopes that even one person might avoid the ordeal he went through.

As the father of a now-grown daughter and grandfather to two grandsons, ages 13 and 14, he also says he respects the sow grizzly's decision to protect her cubs. Her actions, he still believes, were natural, not aggressive. "She wasn't trying to kill me," he says. "She was trying to control the situation."

Just as Ray Walker is doing today.

NATURE MAKES WELL

Roy Campbell was having the time of his life at the start of 2003. The retired butcher and his wife, Heather, were busy spoiling grandchildren, enjoying their many friends, hunting rabbits and waterfowl, fishing, raising elk and red deer, and boating on their home waters of New Zealand's South Island.

But things changed abruptly on January 21. Roy's doctor grimly told him he had cancer of the esophagus and that it was too advanced to operate. Another local doctor agreed. They told him he'd be dead in 9 to 16 months, tops.

Rubbish, Roy declared. At 61, he wasn't ready to leave his boyhood sweetheart, not to mention their kids, grandkids and friends. But something else motivated him to not merely accept the doctors' death sentence: his love of fishing, hunting and the outdoors in general.

So Roy shopped around and found a doctor in Auckland on the North Island who, for a hefty fee, would remove the tumour and rebuild his esophagus with part of his stomach. The operation took place that March, and Roy started chemotherapy a few months later. He dropped from 205 pounds to 140, but survived.

People who have stared down death tend to have a whole

different perspective on life. Some slow down and take it easy. Others see the experience as permission to drive harder, to wring every bit of enjoyment out of life. To the surprise of nobody who knew him, that's what Roy did. Just a year after his operation, Roy and Heather landed in Calgary, where a mutual friend introduced them to me. Over the following few weeks, we fly-fished for trout and toured the Rockies, where they saw their first grizzly. Though still weakened from his cancer ordeal, Roy was upbeat, enthusiastically embracing everything we did. "Just bloody marvellous" was his battle cry.

One day, we fly-fished the Bow River. I landed a couple of nice trout on streamers, and Roy was as happy as if he'd caught them. By the time the sun started to drop, he was obviously tired, but kept casting until he finally hooked a small rainbow. "Just bloody marvellous," he said, slipping the fish back into the water. "Now we can quit."

Five years went by, during which time my wife, Karen, and I visited the Campbells for a once-in-a-lifetime New Zealand adventure. Then in January 2009, cancer returned, this time to Roy's bowels. And again, he was determined to beat it. "I understood it more this time, so it didn't faze me," he says.

Shortly after the ensuing operation, Roy was back hunting from a duck blind – despite a temporary ostomy pouch tucked under his waders. The second bout of cancer only strengthened his resolve to spend time outdoors with family and friends. "It's the friendships I relish most," he says. "People who shoot and fish together have that lovely comradeship going."

And so it was the Campbells returned to Canada last year. Roy and I fished for cooperative salmon off Vancouver Island and for elusive trout on the Sunshine Coast. He caught the largest salmon – 21 pounds – but seemed even happier when I lucked into a 51-pound halibut.

Through it all, Roy never stopped smiling, uttering words of encouragement, asking questions and generally savouring the experience. Even when the wind blew up three-metre swells, he stood solidly on the rolling deck, fighting fish after fish. He was the very embodiment of the adage "The physician heals, Nature makes well."

Then the Campbells and another couple rented a motorhome and hit the Dempster Highway, making a 1500-kilometre round-trip from Dawson City to Inuvik in the Arctic Circle. They even boated down the Mackenzie River to Tuktoyaktuk.

Back in Alberta several weeks later, Roy was still going strong, and whipped my butt shooting clays at a friend's cabin. And the following morning, he returned from sitting in a tree stand to excitedly describe a cow elk he'd seen.

Now pushing 70, Roy continues to live life like there's no tomorrow. He feels blessed to have twice defeated cancer, and talks to people with the disease around the world,

telling them what to expect and helping to buoy their spir-
its. "I've been spared for a reason," he says.

Just bloody marvellous, I'd say.

TOUCHING THE PINE

Touching the Boundary Pine is a rite of spring.

This stooped yet stately limber pine reigns over Grass Pass in the Highwood region of Kananaskis Country west of Longview in southwestern Alberta.

The Boundary Pine was named by R.M. Patterson, Canada's best adventure writer, who packed more thrills and danger into one month of living than most of us do in a lifetime. In the early 1930s, Patterson bought the historic Buffalo Head Ranch. He made the limber pine famous by naming it the Boundary Pine because it marked the southern boundary of his grazing leases.

A photo of the Boundary Pine graces the cover of his 1961 hardcover book, *The Buffalo Head*, in which Patterson describes his ranching days in the Highwood in the 1930s and '40s.

Many years ago, when I read *The Buffalo Head*, which is packed full of local history and raw adventure, I was intrigued by the Boundary Pine and wondered if it still survived after all these years and through the mighty west winds that buffet the region. A bit of research revealed that it did indeed still stand, lone and proud on the edge of the windswept Bull Creek Hills.

After I made a few unsuccessful attempts to find the famous tree, I asked a friend for help. Thanks to his advice and his crudely drawn map, I soon found the Boundary Pine.

The first time I saw it, I was immediately struck that this tree with a crooked and split trunk was still standing tall half a century after R.M. Patterson wrote about it. Life and strength seemed to radiate from its scraggly limbs. As I touched the trunk for the first time, I closed my eyes and tried to imagine all that this tree had experienced in its lifetime.

So started an annual ritual to hike up the rocky Pack Trail Coulee, which inexplicably seems to increase in steepness every year, and touch the Boundary Pine as a gesture of affirmation of life, both mine and the tree's. The hike ranges from 60 to 90 minutes, depending how often you stop to marvel at the surrounding mountains or to scan the flanking hills for signs of wildlife, convenient pauses which allow both heart rate and breathing to return to normal.

Karen and I made the trip this past weekend. The trudge up the coulee trail seemed more challenging than usual – couldn't be our age or winter-weary muscles, could it? – but when we broke into the open and began following a well-worn trail toward the Boundary Pine, my heart started beating faster in anticipation of seeing it again after almost one year.

I wasn't disappointed. The tree still stands, crooked yet

proud, not too different than when Patterson first named it more than eight decades ago. It still exudes a sweet mixture of power and history. The Boundary Pine's bark is rough to the touch, its exposed roots a tangled network of life reaching deep into the earth.

The roots anchor the Boundary Pine. And the tree itself anchors me. I take comfort in the knowledge that it survives.

Being able to touch it every spring provides hope that we can continue our annual visits for a long time to come. As long as the Boundary Pine still stands, all will be okay in the world.

May it ever be so.

NIGHT OF THE WOLVES

I awoke with a start, unsure what had roused me from an already fitful sleep. Then I heard the wolf howl, far away yet clear as a church bell on a spring morning. It was a sorrowful, haunting sound, starting low in tone and rising to a high pitch before it was swallowed up in the star-studded darkness. Immediately, another eerie howl broke the silence, then another.

Soon I could hear the entire pack howling, then individual animals yipping as they drew closer. The pack was on the move. Their hunt had begun.

Simultaneously thrilled and uneasy, I fed another log to the fire and took comfort in the growing glow and heat. And I wondered why the heck I was out there in the isolated forest at midnight, alone except for the wolves and my own misgivings.

I was lying on a bed of green spruce boughs shrouded by a crude lean-to I'd constructed several hours earlier. I had no sleeping bag, no water, no food, no books, no flashlight, no radio, no firearm and no human company.

It was all part of an early-March survival workshop offered by the provincial Fish and Wildlife division at a conservation camp deep in the forestry reserve of west-central

Alberta. The solo camp-out, on a snowy Saturday night with temperatures dropping to minus-ten, was a practical test for 14 participants after several hours of classroom and field instruction on how to survive in the woods.

"Someday, you will use this knowledge," instructor Dave George told the group during the opening night seminar. "If you can survive for 24 hours, you can probably survive for 24 days."

George noted that anybody who spends time in the outdoors – pilots, hikers, anglers, hunters, boaters and backcountry skiers – faces the possibility of an unplanned stay in the wilderness after becoming lost or hurt, or both. I knew from personal experience how easily that could happen.

Twenty years earlier, as a teenager in Winnipeg, I'd become hopelessly lost with a friend after we'd skipped school to go grouse and rabbit hunting in Manitoba's Interlake region. After walking in circles and finally deciding that we didn't have a clue where we were, Paul and I spent a frosty night in the woods, cooking grouse on a spit and taking turns feeding the fire. The highlight of the night was when I fell asleep on my watch and awoke to see my friend's coat on fire from a wayward spark. I quickly helped put him out and apologized, but I don't think he slept much more that night.

The next afternoon, after we'd stupidly spent several more hours wandering aimlessly in the remote, swamp-pocked terrain, we heard a military search and rescue helicopter approaching. It landed in a clearing and picked us up. We were tired, dehydrated, hungry and more than a little red-faced. So getting lost and surviving weren't new to me, but this time I was doing it on purpose.

Dave George promised that spending the night alone in the bush would be "a real character builder." He cautioned all of us to not let our imaginations get carried away during the night. Wildlife like wolves would be deterred by our fires, he said, as would other potentially dangerous animals such as grizzly bears. Even though it was winter, we knew grizzlies can wander out of their dens anytime the urge strikes.

I wasn't sure if George was trying to calm or unnerve us as he described a young woman in a previous solo survival camp who had been unaware that a wolf, under cover of darkness, had crept within ten metres and sat watching her from the trees outside the light of the campfire. The next day, instructors read the story from the wolf's tracks in fresh snow.

Noting there are no documented wolf attacks on people in North America, George warned the students their biggest danger lived in the mind, where lurks the triple threat of loneliness, boredom and fear. People who are lost fear wild animals, hunger, thirst, cold, death and injury and the unknown, also known as the Bogeyman Factor. Sometimes lost people also fear ridicule from peers who might regard them as weak, or punishment from parents and others. (Luckily, my dad and stepmother were away at their cottage at the lake and were unaware I was lost until after I was found – and the military delivered a whopping bill for the helicopter.)

George also told us that most humans can go four days without water and up to 40 days without food. It's most important, he said, to immediately establish some sort of shelter, no matter how crude, and a campfire with plenty of dry wood. Pace yourself, he said. Avoid getting overheated and exhausted. And, whatever you do, don't drink untreated standing water, which might hold a nasty parasitic infection called giardia, which wreaks unpleasant havoc with a person's gastro-intestinal system.

He outlined a simple survival procedure called STOP, an acronym for: Sit down; Think about your predicament; Observe a shelter location, materials and firewood; Practise basic survival skills like building a shelter, campfire and signal fire and setting snares for catching small animals to eat.

After more lectures on building a lean-to and campfire, and how to snare a rabbit, we were driven well back into the forest and dropped off at one-mile intervals. All we had with us were the clothes we were wearing, an axe and a tin survival kit containing snare wire, matches, plastic bags to melt snow for water, tiny cubes of dry boullion and two teabags. Snow was falling as the truck drove away. My emotions were mixed as I watched it disappear down the road.

I spent the next several hours building a lean-to and stockpiling dead wood for both my campfire and an emergency signal fire. I thought I had enough wood for a week. But when a few instructors returned just before dark to make sure I hadn't reconsidered and didn't want to return to base, one of them looked at my woodpile and grimly advised, "Get more wood. It's going to be cold." So I collected more wood until darkness enveloped the forest.

So began a very long night. I was bored. I was lonely, thinking of Karen and the girls, then 7 and 11, back home, reading stories, watching movies, safe and cozy. What were they doing right now? And what the heck was I doing here? Silly as it was, I thought of Sasquatches, crazed axe murderers and, yes, the Bogeyman. I also spent some time remembering being lost in Manitoba, eating charred, half-raw grouse, and Paul's coat catching fire during the night. Somehow I found that last part funnier than I had 20 years ago.

Apart from the wolves, which made my heart beat a little faster for about 20 minutes, the night in the lean-to was relatively uneventful, my wild imagination notwithstanding. I tried sleeping but couldn't manage more than 45 minutes at a time. That was just long enough for the fire to die down, forcing me to restart it several times in the night. I sipped about two tablespoons of snowmelt from a plastic bag that I'd carefully placed a metre away from the fire.

It was overcast and snowing lightly when dawn finally came about at seven a.m. I was hungry and thirsty, but I also felt blessed: I had a wolf story to tell.

Just before noon, a truck horn blasted a few hundred metres away – the instructors' cue for me to light my emergency signal fire within three minutes. I made the deadline, watching with satisfaction as thick black smoke billowed up past the trees. I'd survived the experience, and learned a few life lessons.

Yet as I walked down the cutline toward the truck, I couldn't shake the feeling that the next survival test might not be a drill.

KINSHIP

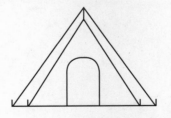

ONE LAST CAST

She stands knee-deep in the water, silhouetted in the sunset's waning glow.

It's so dark she can no longer see her fly on the water. But still she casts, gracefully and confidently, hopeful for one last trout.

Her father watches silently, proud yet a little sad, as he kneels on the nearby bank. He wills a trout to take the fly, to provide sweet icing for this last outing before their lives change forever.

But it is not to be. "Time to go," he tells her. "Just one more cast," she replies. "Just one more cast."

The father smiles. He recalls the first time she uttered those words. It was on their first fishing trip together, 15 years ago.

She was just two and one-half years old when they were invited to fish a stocked farm dugout. She helped her father dig the worms in the garden, then eagerly pitched in to pack the gear. Bubbling with excitement as the rods were rigged up, she insisted on casting her own after he showed her how.

She shrieked with joy when the first trout hit her bait, almost wrenching the rod from her tiny hands. Her first fish.

An angler was born; the father had a new fishing partner and a fresh outlook on a sport he'd loved since childhood. The circle was complete.

When it came time to leave the dugout, that little girl said – for the first of many times to come – those four words that are beautiful music to a parent who fishes: "Just one more cast."

The father packed up and still she sat, big brown eyes transfixed on the bobber floating on the pond's surface. When she finally, and reluctantly, got in the car, she re-counted the outing all the way home, then provided her mother with a detailed narrative about each fish.

Over the next 15 years, father and daughter fished to-gether regularly, sharing conversations about fish and life, spectacular terrain, wildlife encounters – the trio of swimming moose at that high alpine lake was a once-in-a-lifetime highlight – cold dunkings, sunsets and other rich experiences which malls and video arcades can't provide.

She developed a deep concern for clean water, litter-free banks, healthy fish and habitat, fishing ethics and wildlife. Her commitment to catch-and-release became so absolute she'd good-naturedly rebuke her dad for keeping the odd brook trout for lunch.

While her skills and confidence grew, many of her ques-tions tested her father's knowledge of fishing and the out-doors. He answered them as well as he could, but knew many responses fell short.

When her younger sister was old enough to join them on outings, she eagerly helped teach her how to fish. Together, they'd catch night crawlers by flashlight in the backyard the night before a walleye-fishing trip. They delighted in holding up writhing double handfuls of the slimy critters, then knocking on the window to get the attention of their mother, who hates night crawlers.

Three years and many trips to lakes, ponds and small creeks after her farm pond initiation, the father one day thought his oldest daughter was ready for a larger river. After helping set up his 5-year-old partner on the riverbank overlooking a deep hole full of promise, he started casting his own line a few yards away. That's when she informed him, sweetly but firmly, that he would have to move because this was her spot.

After she got into fly-fishing at age 11, the daughter and father hiked into a high mountain lake renowned for its feisty cutthroat trout. She wasted no time rigging up. Before he'd made his first cast, she'd released three trout hooked on a dry fly.

Once, they reluctantly agreed not to bring fishing tackle on a group hike to a pretty set of waterfalls on a clear mountain stream. But the plan changed when they got there. Several brookies were rising to eat hatching insects. The daughter insisted on breaking out flies, split shot and fishing line from the survival kit, then promptly landed a trout with the emergency tackle tied to a willow branch.

One spring, she caught a 20-inch bull trout, the biggest the father had seen. She gently cradled the fish in the water, reassuring it of its safety with soft, soothing words, until it regained enough strength to swim away.

A few years ago, the father noticed his daughter was changing. A little girl no more, she started fishing apart from him, politely but firmly declining advice about fly selection, where to cast and just about everything else.

This sense of independence grew stronger in everything she did, from schoolwork to social life and all things in between. A confident, self-motivated young woman had emerged, seemingly overnight.

When darkness finally chased her off the river the night of that final outing, she insisted on driving her father home, the first time ever after a fishing trip. Silently, he wrestled with feelings of sadness, joy and pride.

As they travel this morning to the University of Lethbridge, where the biological sciences program should provide many answers her father couldn't, he'll face similar emotions.

And he'll wish they'd shared just one more cast before she left.

WALKING AWAY

Life's lessons come when we least expect them. That truism has never resonated so clearly as on a beautiful summer evening many years ago.

I'd invited our younger daughter, Sarah, aged 11, to go fly-fishing on a pretty little trout stream near our home in southwestern Alberta. It would be a rare outing without her older sister Chelsea, at 14 already a pretty good fly-fisher.

Sarah accepted, but with obvious apprehension. I asked her what was wrong, and the truth emerged.

Karen and I had given Sarah her first fly rod as a birthday present a few months earlier. The gift represented a graduation of sorts, a milestone in her development as an angler.

Like her sister, Sarah had fished since she was a toddler, first with bait for northern pike and walleye, eventually moving on to artificial flies for trout and Arctic grayling.

But she'd always used a spinning rod and reel, which are much easier to cast. Anyone who has ever tried casting a fly with a long, whippy fly rod for the first time knows it can be a challenge.

There are so many things to remember: let the line straighten on the forward and back cast, keep the rod pointed between imaginary ten and two o'clock positions, straighten the forearm, maintain a fluid movement and don't overexert.

Sarah's initial outings with her new fly rod were frustrating. The line became entangled, flies caught in bushes or snapped off on rocks, and rain and strong winds sabotaged her most valiant attempts.

My persistent streamside coaching hadn't helped. The perfectionist in me was upset at my inability to teach Sarah how to do it right. I was becoming just as frustrated.

But that summer evening was a perfect time to try again. Conditions were ripe for Sarah's first trout on her fly rod.

The wind was calm, the sky clear and blue. The surface of the clear creek was dimpled with eastern brook trout rising to devour mayflies, caddis flies and other insects off the surface. Sarah and I both expressed hope she'd catch a brookie that night.

After quickly rigging up, we set off upstream. I stayed close to Sarah, pointing out rising fish and giving her advice on how to cast her tiny mayfly imitation to maximize chances of a strike. Alas, most of Sarah's casts were too short, too long or just plain landed wrong.

We continued to encounter rising brook trout as we moved along the creek. But Sarah's frustration was visibly mounting after each miscast or tangle. I offered advice in what I hoped was an encouraging way, but it wasn't working.

As we walked on the gravel shoreline toward a nice pool, I suddenly spotted a black bear emerge from the trees on the other side of the creek, about a football field's length away. Sarah and I remained motionless while we quietly watched it.

Although our family was accustomed to seeing deer, elk, moose and other wildlife on our outdoor adventures – and considered each viewing a bonus – we'd never had a bear that close.

As it ambled away, Sarah worriedly asked if we should head back to the vehicle. Just as I assured her we were safe and should return to fishing, the bear vanished in the trees. I smiled, recalling that First Nations people consider bears a good omen.

Sure enough, we'd walked only a short distance when I spotted a chunky brook trout feeding below an overhanging willow bush on the far side of the creek. I knew it was a bigger fish by the way it sipped almost imperceptibly, barely breaking the glasslike surface, while smaller trout nearby splashed or even jumped clear of the water in their zeal to eat bugs.

Sarah's first cast was short by about six feet, and her second was too far ahead by about four. On her third cast, the rod dropped too low on the back cast and her fly caught on a root protruding from the shoreline rocks on the shoreline.

Several missed casts later, the trout was still rising but Sarah was so frustrated she was ready to quit. That's when it dawned on me that perhaps my presence was doing more harm than good.

I asked Sarah if I should leave her alone.

"Yes, that's a good idea," Sarah replied, quickly adding, "I can do this, you know."

"I know you can," I said.

I turned and walked away, wading upstream through a shallow riffle with my eye on a promising pool dotted with rising trout. Suddenly I heard Sarah whoop with joy.

I turned around just in time to see a trout jump clear of the water. It was attached to Sarah's fly line. Her rod was doubled over.

By the time I got back, the fight was almost over. I helped Sarah net the beautiful foot-long trout. As she took it in her hands, her smile under large aviator-type sunglasses extended ear to ear.

Gently, she eased the trout back in the water and watched as it swam away.

With great excitement, Sarah described how she'd managed to put a perfect cast over the trout within seconds of my departure. She'd seen it rise to her fly and set the hook perfectly.

"I knew I could do it," Sarah said, still beaming.

My happiness matched hers. But suddenly I felt somewhat subdued, like I'd just simultaneously made a life-defining discovery and witnessed a significant rite of passage. Sarah's persistence had paid off. She'd done it on her own, without fatherly advice.

Sarah had taught me a valuable lesson, one that I will

never forget as she and Chelsea travel through their life journeys.

I'd learned daughters are for fathers to cherish, to nurture, to encourage and to protect when younger.

But at some point fathers must make the hardest decision of them all. We must know when to walk away – to let our daughters spread their wings and figure out life on their own, without our constant harping in the background.

That's the way it is, the way it should be and how it always will be.

THE CREEK

We call it The Creek. It is a place of solace, of beauty, of promise and of joy. Born at the foot of the Rocky Mountains, it is a small stream, in places narrow enough to jump across and shallow enough to wade in old sneakers. Karen, Chelsea, Sarah and I possessively consider The Creek our own. It's a grandly egocentric notion, to be sure, but one that we cannot shake, for we know it intimately, as a lifelong friend.

We have camped in a rustic streamside campground where tawny-coated whitetail deer grazed in the pinkish hue of the early morning sun. We have hiked beside its meandering, sparkling waters. We've thrown sticks in the water for our dog, Belle, then laughed as she drenched us with cold water shaken off her black coat. In winter, we have strapped on skis and glided on the snow beside The Creek, stopping to build a fire when the cold made fingers numb and boots had to be removed to rub feeling back into frozen feet. We have cycled down the valley, dodging rocks, ground squirrel holes and the occasional cow pie and bear poop.

Especially, though, The Creek is where we have spent more hours than anyone deserves casting flies for the plentiful eastern brook trout that live there. The girls learned to fly-fish here, after graduating from spin-fishing with bait in lakes. They liked it especially because the furred and feathered flies were pretty and it was fun to get in the water to meet the fish in their element. The Creek is where they shed tears of frustration and fought to focus while fine-tuning their casting skills with supple graphite rods and light nylon tippet that the devilish wind would conspire to tangle in the willows along the bank.

The Creek was where the girls and I fished together while Karen patiently watched, read a book, played with Belle or took pictures. We three fly-fishers spent countless hours trying to entice the small, gorgeous trout to give us a few minutes of excitement before we played God. Whenever a hooked trout struggled in our hands, we always discussed whether to gently release or kill it and take it back to camp to cook on a forked willow branch over the fire, like a smokie with fins. The girls never killed trout they'd catch in The Creek. Yet they eagerly roasted any that I chose to keep, the process generally preceded by comments like, "Sorry, trout, that you are dead, and thank you for your life, but you sure taste good."

In springtime, The Creek undergoes a transformation that is at once cleansing and violent. In the few weeks after ice-out – when warm temperatures and winds have peeled back the water's icy seal – the current runs clear and shallow. Velvety pussy willows sprout on the bank. But the gentle flow of early spring dramatically changes when the hot sunshine is extinguished by heavy rainfalls, rapidly melting the winter snowpack in the headwater's valleys, forests and alpine meadows. When that happens, great gushes of water rage down The Creek, turning it into a raging muddy torrent that spills over the banks, flushing out silt and deadfall, before the water returns to lower levels and increased clarity.

One such spring, a powerful flood hit the valley and The Creek turned wilder than anybody could remember. Like molten lava, deep, cocoa-coloured water swept relentlessly over the valley, tearing out wooden bridges, uprooting mighty pines and rolling boulders the size of small cars along like bowling balls. Downstream communities sustained severe damage. Cows, sheep, deer and other wildlife drowned. A few days after the flood subsided, our family visited The Creek to see if it was okay. It wasn't. Struck speechless by what we saw, we silently scanned the devastated valley from our vehicle, and then got out for a closer look. Broken tree trunks jutted from the banks. The rocks were covered in a thick, sandy silt. Familiar trail signs were gone.

But what really struck us was that The Creek itself had moved – in places almost 100 metres – to a new channel the flood had carved in the valley floor. An old, rutted logging road that used to run along one side of The Creek now straddled it. In silence, we surveyed the evidence of how nature's raw power had transformed the valley. Suddenly, Sarah and Chelsea – then 10 and 13, respectively – clambered over the rocks to where the streambed had been just a few weeks earlier. Seconds later, with shrill shouts of alarm, they beckoned Karen and me to join them.

The girls were standing beside a foot-deep pool of water barely two metres square. Before the flood, it had been part of The Creek's main stem; now it was an orphaned pool, cut off from the flowing water and destined to dry up within a few weeks. At first glance, the pool looked barren of life, but the girls knew differently.

"Look," Chelsea said, pointing frantically. "There's a trout."

I followed the path of her finger to the middle of the pool. A brightly spotted brook trout seven inches long swam slowly over the rocks lining the bottom. A slow scan of the rest of the pool revealed several more small trout.

"Won't they die?" asked Sarah, brown eyes wide with concern.

"Yes, they will," I replied. "If predators don't get them, the water will soon be gone and they will die."

Both girls became pensive, their faces dark with sorrow and thought.

"We'll save them," pronounced Chelsea, with a familiar determined tone that I knew meant there was no stopping her.

"Let's get going," Sarah instantly added.

At that, the girls waded into the pool and, after a splashing flurry of missed chances, each scooped up a trout with their hands. Then, gently cradling the fish in their hands, they ran over to the newly-formed channel. After kneeling at the edge of the flowing water, they lowered the trout in a calm back eddy. They waited patiently for the fish to regain their strength before opening their hands and watched them swim into the current. Then the girls bolted back to the pool to try to save the rest.

All afternoon, Sarah and Chelsea hurried from stranded pool to stranded pool, hand-catching dozens of trapped trout and releasing them into the flowing water. Plastic bags that once held sandwiches in the girls' backpacks eventually were recruited for the rescue operation. The bags were filled with water, and the trout – like goldfish going home from a pet store – were carried in them overland to the stream – and freedom.

At one point, I stood silently in wonder, marvelling at our daughters' compassion and determination to save the otherwise doomed trout. One day, we hoped to catch – maybe even eat – some of these trout. But I knew the girls' motivation went far beyond that short-sighted goal. They felt it was their mission to give the fish a chance. Nature's way would have been to let the trout die in their disconnected pools, their flesh nourishing insects, birds and animals – the whole circle-of-life thing. The girls, however, would have none of it. Not this time.

Watching them running back and forth, moving trout

after trout from pool to stream, I couldn't help pondering how this moment had come to be, the paths they'd taken that led to their selfless act of salvation. At that stage of their lives, we'd been exploring nature together for several years. Starting when they were old enough to understand, we had discussed together the need to be environmentally responsible, to take care of nature, to respect it.

The girls had fished since they were toddlers, when I introduced them to an activity that I'd loved since I was a kid. Fishing brought back pleasant memories from an oft-troubled childhood and had helped me through stretches of personal rough waters. I was an adult before I really understood the healing power of nature, and our role in it, and how fishing was about much more than just catching fish.

Watching the girls that day, I knew they'd already made that connection. They'd learned much more than I had by their age. This natural classroom had taught them well.

We call it The Creek.

IN SPIRIT

The Cessna 185 taxied away from the dock, picked up speed along the water and lifted effortlessly into the bright blue northern Ontario sky. Soon it was out of sight. In a few seconds, even the drone of the motor was swallowed by the wilderness. Silence returned to the remote lake.

"Well, here we are," my brother Rick said to nobody in particular.

"Yeah, we sure are," I answered.

To anyone listening, our simple verbal exchange might have sounded rather lame. In truth, though, it held a much deeper meaning – neither of us could really believe we were indeed *here*, miles away from civilization, standing on a dock as waves lapped against it.

Rick and I had dreamed of doing a trip like this together for more than 30 years. We'd talked about it, we'd agreed it would be fun, but we'd never got around to doing it. Several years ago, the plan expanded to include our dad, Bob, and Rick's son, Dan. It would be an all-guys getaway to catch a few fish, tell some lies and try to bridge the gap created by busy lives and three provinces. But that's as far as it ever went – talk.

Then, in 2003, Dad died in a car accident at the age of

82. One key member of our planned trip was gone, and it seemed destined never to happen. But both Rick and I underestimated the vision and determination of Dan, who, at age 24, knew more about motivation than Rick and I ever will.

Two summers earlier, Dan and a friend had ventured to northern Ontario's Devlin Lake, where they enjoyed almost non-stop action for walleye and pike. A photo of Dan with a 39-inch pike even graces the website of Wilderness Air, which runs the outpost at Devlin Lake as part of a string of fly-in fishing operations. What better place, he thought, for the elusive all-guys getaway?

And so it was that we found ourselves standing on the dock at Devlin Lake last August, finally on the fishing trip of our dreams. With the plane gone, we carried our gear up to the rustic but comfortable log cabin and unpacked. Then it was right down to the boat, with tackle boxes, rods, nets and lifejackets in tow.

Soon Dan was piloting us to one of his favourite fishing spots, about ten minutes away. It was a relatively shallow area, with a white plastic buoy marking the location of a giant rock that had likely claimed a few propellers over the years.

We started off using bottom bouncers and spinners, baited with dead minnows. After about five minutes of drifting with the motor turned off, Dan got the first bite. "I've got one," he announced. And he did – a nice chunky walleye. Soon, Rick and I were also watching our rods bounce under the weight of hefty fish.

For several exciting and entertaining minutes, it seemed as though at least one of us would have a nice walleye on. And every now and then someone would also catch a pike, just to liven things up. Then, when the action would start to slow down, we would just move to another spot and start all over again.

Before we knew it, it was late afternoon and our stomachs were telling us it had been a long time since lunch. We reeled in our lines and motored back to camp.

I volunteered to clean the few walleye we'd kept for supper, and pulled out Dad's old wood-handled filleting knife. I'd watched him clean hundreds of fish with that finely honed blade over the years, and I considered it an honour to have it with us. It just seemed so right to be using his favourite fish knife on this trip of a lifetime – one he would have been on if only we'd done it sooner.

And as I sliced off the fillets and removed the skin and cheeks from each of the walleye, it even felt as if Dad's hand was guiding me.

In a way, he hadn't missed the trip after all.

STARTING THEM YOUNG

It was a glorious fall afternoon, with the drab green foliage of trees and willows transformed into dazzling displays of yellows and red.

I often think that if seasons were people, autumn would be the wildly eccentric relative you love to visit. There's nothing subdued or boring about fall. Going strictly on looks, the other three seasons are relatively lacklustre. Autumn's colours are vivid and varied, bursting from nature's palette in a remarkable celebration of brilliant contrasts. Autumn is my favourite season, no question.

But as I drove through the mountains west of the foothills town where we live, I was amazed by what I saw in the various cars and family vans that I met. Even though most of them held children, few kids were actually seeing Mother Nature's spectacular show. Young faces were glued to movies playing on video monitors hanging above them. Children were looking down, apparently reading or, more likely, playing with some kind of computer game, oblivious to the fall magic playing out around them. In surprisingly few vehicles, young passengers actually paid attention to the view outside. Even many adult passengers seemed to be otherwise occupied.

To me, the experience was just another symptom of an ever-growing malaise that threatens the future of our great outdoors: many children either aren't getting the chance to experience nature, or they don't know how to appreciate it even if they do venture out. Recent studies have shown that increased urbanization, the popularity of video games, the growth of single-parent families and a general disinterest all have contributed to a decline in the number of kids in developed countries enjoying the outdoors.

In a cleverly perceptive – and more than slightly tongue-in-cheek – column in *The New Yorker* magazine last March, writer Ellis Weiner introduced readers to a new "astounding multipurpose activity platform" that he called GOING OUTSIDE, which he said would "revolutionize how you spend your time."

"GOING OUTSIDE is not a game or a program, not a device or an app, not a protocol or an operating system," Weiner wrote. "Instead, it's a comprehensive experiential mode that lets you perceive and do things firsthand, without any intervening media or technology."

Among its many benefits, Weiner points out, GOING OUTSIDE enables "complete interactivity with inanimate objects, animals and Nature. Enjoy the texture of real grass, listen to authentic birds, or discover a flower that has grown up out of the earth. By GOING OUTSIDE you'll be astounded by the number and variety of things there are in the world."

Using modern computer language to highlight the benefits of being outside is both enlightening and slightly disturbing. So many of us, adults and children alike, are finding ourselves increasingly engaged in a techno-land of pixels, downloads, instant messaging and apps for every occasion. But along the path to this online fantasy world we risk losing touch with what's very real and important in the natural world around us.

Many adults are willing to make that trade-off, but it behooves all of us to make sure children have every chance to be outdoors. And what if they don't, you might ask?

Well, for starters, they're being robbed of a chance to appreciate a world beyond classrooms, shopping malls, the Internet and other places where a natural sense of wonder seldom exists. By not having a chance to hike, fish, camp and develop a relationship with nature, they aren't discovering where they fit into the grand scheme of things and how their actions can impact natural places and wild things. And without that level of stewardship awareness on the part of our future policy makers, how can we hold out much hope for what lies ahead?

Thankfully, there is hope. There is hope in the dedicated adults – including single parents I know – who still take kids outdoors, and in many organizations such as Guides, Cubs and Scouts, Junior Forest Wardens and various others that teach outdoor education through hands-on experiences. I've had the honour of being involved in several such organizations, including with Chelsea and Sarah when they were younger. But the foundation was laid well before they were old enough to belong to any group.

Starting when they needed to be carried in a pack while hiking or pulled on a sled while we cross-country skied, Karen and I shared with them the wonders of the outdoors. They learned to identify animals and birds but, more importantly, they learned to love seeing them in their natural habitat, and came to appreciate their own respective places in the world.

At age 2, they both started learning not only how to catch fish, but also about the different types, and the places where fish lived. Along the way they learned to respect the rules we had to follow and understand why we didn't litter or otherwise harm their environment. Through fishing they also learned a lot about themselves.

One spring Saturday, on Sarah's 7th birthday, we took her and several other young girls on a nature scavenger hunt. As we walked a mountain trail, they busied themselves finding paper and other litter, pine cones, wildflowers, animal droppings and other "prizes". Garbage was the only prize they were allowed to pick. They spotted squirrels and birds, giggled and competed to see who could collect the most litter. Later, Sarah proclaimed it her favourite birthday party yet.

We camped with our daughters starting from when they were very young, and picnicked in all four seasons. We cross-country skied and hiked. Sarah even hunted deer, ducks and grouse with me, before deciding hunting wasn't for her. We frequented places where they saw wildlife such as deer, elk, moose and bear. We made a game of spotting animals from the car, with a nebulous prize (a candy bar, the first drink of water when we got home, or maybe a hug?) going to the child who saw the first deer, or coyote.

They both developed not just an appreciation of nature, but a love for it that remains strong today as they are well into adulthood. When they both moved to a major West Coast city, they insisted on packing their fly-fishing gear. Karen told me a few minutes ago that Sarah planned to go canoeing with a friend today.

We didn't just raise two daughters. With considerable pride, I can say we raised responsible young people who care about the environment, whose love of wild places and wild creatures is core to who they are.

There's no question that people who are introduced to the outdoors as youngsters become its biggest allies later in life. And with Nature under constant siege on many fronts, it needs all the friends it can get.

UPCOUNTRY

The marsh is ablaze in autumn glory. Thick stands of soft maple trees with leaves of flaming scarlet reflect a perfect mirror image on the still water. A great blue heron floats by at treetop level, while a turkey vulture carves circles in the deep blue sky far overhead. A soft whisper breaks the early morning silence.

"You know, I could never get tired of seeing this," says Monte Hummel, a broad smile creasing his tanned face. "This is how I imagine Heaven to be."

Indeed, this is Hummel's *other* world, one far removed from his busy office in downtown Toronto, where he guides the operation of World Wildlife Fund Canada, part of the world's largest independent conservation organization.

On this sunny, crisp mid-week morning in October 2002, he is walking on his 270-acre property in the remote backwoods along the Canadian Shield northwest of Kingston, Ontario. Instead of the sports jacket and casual pants he'd be wearing if he were in his Toronto office, Hummel is clad in khaki pants, heavy-soled hiking boots and a red-and-black plaid shirt.

Hummel loves this land. He calls it "upcountry," but it's clear this is his paradise, a life-affirming refuge where his strong personal beliefs and conservation philosophy are validated by nature itself.

His simple A-frame cabin, topped with a lichen-encrusted shingled roof, overlooks Loon Lake, a forest-ringed, bathtub-shaped piece of water just one kilometre long. The cabin has no power or telephone and is heated with a cast-iron wood-burning stove. There is no running water. Hummel fetches pails of water from the lake, breaking ice in winter. An old leaky aluminum rowboat stashed on shore is pressed into service whenever Hummel decides to fish for largemouth bass, gaining both a meal and some exercise by bailing and rowing.

Hummel, 56, comes to Loon Lake to rejuvenate spiritually, mentally and physically. He observes nature, snowshoes, hikes, hunts ducks and ruffed grouse, writes, reflects and plans. Although much of his time there is spent alone, he's sometimes joined by his two grown children, Robin and Doug, and his wife, Sherry Pettigrew, my first cousin and a respected conservationist and author in her own right.

Hummel's goal is to spend a few days each month at his cabin, and longer in spring and autumn. In his 1999 book about Loon Lake, *Wintergreen*, he muses: "My greatest regret, after 30 years in the Canadian and world conservation movement, is that I have not taken more time to experience what we have all worked so hard to protect. Because without dipping back into our source regularly, any of us can lose our way." For Hummel, Loon Lake is a key *source*.

Being motivated when it comes to conservation issues has never been a problem for Hummel. He's been in the forefront of the campaign for more than 30 years, beginning with Pollution Probe, which he co-founded in 1969 after learning his favourite boyhood fishing hole, the English River north of Kenora in northern Ontario, had become poisoned by mercury from a pulp and paper plant. The river had been an important economic source for the local Ojibway people, and its contamination led to social, economic and personal depression. That issue, Hummel wrote in *Wintergreen*, "did more to propel me into a career of environmentalism than any other single event in my life."

In 1978, Hummel moved to the Toronto-based World Wildlife Fund Canada, where he was executive director until he became president in 1985. When he joined WWF, it had an annual budget of $110,000 and two full-time employees. Today, it employs 75 people with a budget of $12.5-million. It is one of 27 groups within the international WWF, which employs 3,500 and raises half a billion dollars annually for projects designed to stop environmental degradation and build a future in which people live in harmony with nature. WWF has more than 60,000 supporters in Canada.

In Canada, WWF counts among its proudest accomplishments: completion of a North Atlantic right whale recovery plan in partnership with the federal Department of

Fisheries and Oceans; development of an integrated management program with a group of Ontario apple growers, which reduced their use of toxic pesticides; and completion of the ten-year Endangered Spaces campaign, which resulted in the establishment of more than 1,000 new parks, wilderness areas and nature reserves, more than doubling the amount of protected area in Canada.

In 2000, Hummel was appointed an officer of the Order of Canada in recognition of his long-standing commitment to conservation. In the past three decades, he has served on the boards of more than 30 Canadian and international conservation organizations, and has been an advisor to numerous government panels. He's one of the first conservation leaders to encourage the involvement of corporations in habitat protection.

Hummel also works closely with other national conservation groups, including Ducks Unlimited Canada. Gord Edwards, DU's executive director, says the relationship is built on mutual respect.

Edwards says it's important that the two organizations continue to work together. A collaborative approach toward their conservation mandate has become a much more effective way for DU to do business, he notes. Working alongside organizations like WWF allows the pooling of financial resources and steers two large volunteer and membership groups toward common goals, Edwards adds.

"As an added bonus, we gain from Monte Hummel's

leadership and extensive experience in the conservation community," he says. "With the huge challenges that like-minded conservation organizations are facing today, we need to pull together whenever possible."

At Loon Lake that October day, Hummel stops often as he traverses the terrain, identifying bird calls and wildflowers and inspecting animal droppings. He scampers up rocky ridges, stopping to cock an ear toward the sound of a flushing grouse. He promises to try to call a wolf that evening, just to see if he can get one to howl back. At a beaver pond covered in brightly coloured fallen leaves, he points out a sign he made noting the presence of Blanding's turtles, a threatened species. He shows where he's seen otters frolic on the ice in winter, and where he spied a pair of wood ducks a few weeks ago.

One morning, the rising sun cast a mystical light over a beaver pond while ducks sped past overhead. Hummel rested his five-foot-ten-inch frame on a poplar stump. When it was time to leave, he became pensive, his somber mood as clearly reflected on his ruddy face as the trees were mirrored on the pond's glassy surface. To Hummel, the pond has special meaning. A few years earlier, he scattered the ashes of his father, Solon, on a small island. Back in 1988, he placed the ashes of a favourite Labrador retriever, Walter, along the pond's shoreline. "I always get a little emotional at this spot," Hummel says.

Autumn is Hummel's favourite season, and October his

preferred month. In *Wintergreen*, Hummel writes that fall at Loon Lake is tinged in sadness. Yet, he is quick to add, it is the type of sadness he yearns to feel.

> I find myself stopping more frequently along the trail, and lingering longer. I remember things from the past and reflect on their meaning … Perhaps it is because this season is so unimaginably beautiful and so deeply personal.
> Or perhaps it is because fall is when the land speaks straight to our hearts.

Hummel plans to never stop listening to the land and heeding its message.

A SPECIAL TIME
AND PLACE

July 2001. The drone of an outboard motor broke the early-morning silence as an aluminum boat sliced through the calm water toward us. Standing on the dock, surrounded by a small mountain of luggage, coolers and rod cases, Sarah and I watched the boat. Suddenly, my heart started racing, my mind rewinding to a special summer of my youth, 31 years ago. I was 17, just one year older than Sarah was now, when I stood on the same dock on the same northern Manitoba lakeshore and waited for a boat to appear, to carry me into an exciting, life-defining adventure. Now, more than three decades later, I was back, to reconnect with the past, relive memories and forge new ones with a daughter who'd surprisingly agreed to indulge her father's dream by travelling 1830 kilometres with him to share his sentimental journey. I looked at Sarah, grinned a crooked grin and muttered, "This is it."

Brown eyes gleaming brightly, Sarah smiled back. Then, in infinite teenaged wisdom, she gently cautioned, "Remember, Dad. Don't make too much out of this trip."

She reminded me of our deal. Sarah was a reluctant

participant on this trip. Like many 16-year-old girls, her idea of a good time was the West Edmonton Mall or a Nelly Furtado concert, not accompanying her middle-aged father on a sentimental journey. She'd expressed concern that the experience would drip with rampant mushiness every minute, as I reconnected with the past and attached special significance to every detail. Sarah agreed to come only when I promised I'd try to keep my feelings to myself.

So when Sarah cautioned me not to make too much of the trip, I knew I had to at least try to keep up my end of the bargain.

★ ★ ★

It was winter 1970. In a few months, I would finish Grade 11 in Winnipeg. I was a typically brash and rebellious 17-year-old, confused and angry at the world over my mother's prolonged death from cancer two years earlier. I was desperate to escape. I knew I had to get away – from my family and friends, from the city, from the memories that kept crashing in on me from nowhere.

A summer job seemed like the best choice. Lacking in ambition and most useful skills, all I really knew was that I was happiest when traipsing around outdoors with my dad and younger brother, fishing for walleye and northern pike and yellow perch, or hunting for spruce and ruffed grouse. When I wasn't actually outdoors, I lived to read about it. With money earned painting fences and mowing lawns, I bought magazines that took me to faraway places. Through the pages of Outdoor

Life, Sports Afield *and* Field & Stream, *I caught* LUNKER!!! *bass in Alabama, stalked* MONSTER!!! *brown bears in Alaska and pursued* MAN-EATING!!! *tigers in India.*

While leafing through the back pages of an old Field & Stream one day, I found a bank of advertisements for far-off sporting lodges catering to well-off anglers and hunters. Some were in northern Manitoba, which seemed sufficiently far away at the time. I fired off several letters of application. Every day, I rushed home from school to check the mail. For several weeks, nothing.

Then, finally, a letter came from Chicago businessman Dale Hudson, who ran a rustic fishing camp on Elbow Lake, a remote fly- and boat-in spot northeast of Cranberry Portage, more than 800 kilometres north of Winnipeg. He offered me a summer job involving many chores, from cleaning fish and mowing lawns to chopping wood and gassing up the outboards. In my off-hours I could fish. I was ecstatic. What more could a kid want?

That's how it came to be that on a morning in late June 1970 I was standing on a dock in the northern town of Cranberry Portage, waiting for the arrival of a boat to transport me 42 kilometres to Elbow Lake. When I noticed a boat approaching, there was only one person in it. I was expecting Dale Hudson, whom I'd met in Winnipeg a month earlier while he was en route north. I was surprised to see that the man in the boat wasn't my new boss.

This guy was well over six feet, rail-thin, with a wispy patch of thinning brown hair atop a head distinguished by crooked, nicotine-stained teeth and an equine nose. After I helped him tie up the boat, he nodded at me and curtly said, "You must be Bruce. I'm Henry Bradley. Let's get going." Few other words were exchanged as we loaded my duffel and fishing tackle into the boat.

For the next 90 minutes, Henry expertly cut the boat across wind-chopped waves on a chain of three lakes called First, Second and Third Cranberry. My hands clutched the wooden boat seat. My head swivelled, owl-like, as I tried to take in all the sights at once: the forest-covered mainland, rock-studded islands, ducks, gulls, ospreys and white pelicans. It was like a dream. I felt like a farm kid in New York City. For the first of many times that summer, I thought: "This is incredible." We travelled along several kilometres of the serpentine Grass (locals call it the Grassy) River, a narrow strip of water that snaked between tree-studded shorelines lined with tall reeds and submerged logs. We coasted underneath a tar-black wooden railway bridge, and I wondered where the line could possibly go.

Leaving the river for the last time, we entered the broad expanse of open water that was Elbow Lake. We headed due north, following the west shore. Although there were two fishing camps on the lake, I saw no sign of either. Nothing but trees, rocks and water. This, I thought, is really remote. Finally, after rounding a rocky point on our left, I had my first look at the camp that would be my summer refuge.

★ ★ ★

The same view greeted Sarah and me on a sunny July morning 31 years later. The boat in which we were riding was piloted not by Henry Bradley but by Stan Wilson, latest owner of the Big Four Wilderness Camp.

Stan had forewarned me that some things had changed in three decades, particularly after a massive forest fire swept through the region in 1989, destroying all five guest cabins, the main cabin and the ice house. Miraculously, the blaze somehow spared the outhouses and fish-cleaning shack. Stan and his wife, Joan, rebuilt the camp the next spring and were back in business that summer. Now, apart from black spikes of charred tree trunks jutting up from the surrounding pine, poplar and birch forest, it didn't look so different.

Five wood-sided guest cabins, all elevated by concrete pilings, were evenly spaced along a grassy shoreline. I used to cut that grass, I thought. To the west of the cabins was the Wilsons' summer home, the ice house and the same screened fish-cleaning shack where I swatted mosquitoes like a young man possessed while filleting hundreds of walleye in the summer of '70.

My eyes were drawn to a dirty-white clapboard shack nestled in the trees a few hundred yards west of the Big Four camp. Henry Bradley's old trapper's cabin. Last time I saw it, the ground was covered in four feet of snow, and smoke curled out the stovepipe chimney. That was in the winter of 1972. A year and a half after my summer at the fishing camp, I'd spent five weeks helping Henry tend his trapline and care for his sled dogs and learning more about nature – and myself – than I ever could in Winnipeg. But I'm getting ahead of myself.

Now, no smoke came from the chimney. Even from a distance, the cabin looked abandoned and ill-kept. Screaming gulls lifted off a lakeshore rocky outcrop in front of the building. As Stan throttled down the boat to approach the dock, I raised my binoculars to focus in on a boulder cairn perched on the rock. Stan had already told me about that cairn. It was a memorial for my old friend Henry. He died in 1982, just ten years after I'd wintered with him at Elbow Lake.

"I'd like to have to have a closer look at that," I told Sarah.

She grinned, nodded knowingly and rolled her eyes, as if to say, "Here we go."

★ ★ ★

I'd been at the camp for almost two weeks before Henry Bradley invited me fishing. I jumped at the chance because, after all, Henry was the camp's official guide. He knew a lot about fishing Elbow Lake – and just about everything else of interest to an outdoorsy kid.

Henry was a bachelor farmer from the Swan River region of west-central Manitoba. After he put the crop in each spring, he'd head north to his little cabin at Elbow Lake and guide visiting anglers until it was time to go home for harvest. Then, he'd return to Elbow with eight sled dogs, shoot a moose for meat and spend a solo winter trapping. His closest neighbour was 20 kilometres away.

Although I thought I knew a thing or two about fishing for walleye, I discovered our first time out how little that was. Henry's fishing gear – an old fibreglass rod with a battered spinning reel – belied his expertise. After anchoring, I began tying on a wire leader. Henry stopped me, suggesting I tie directly to the jig. "But pike will bite it off," I protested. "True, but you'll catch more pickerel," he replied, patiently. "Trust me."

Henry was right. He caught his first golden-flanked walleye about a minute later. We landed dozens of walleye in a few hours, releasing most and taking a few back to camp for breakfast. Henry also taught me how to safely hand-land walleye and northern pike. That first evening, and every time we fished together after that, Henry always knew exactly where the walleye and big pike would be found. He never missed.

The education didn't end at fishing. Henry had a passion for the place, for the forest and the wildlife that lived there. He would point out and identify passing waterfowl and reverently describe the moose, caribou and wolves that lived in the region. Carefully rolling a cigarette with one hand, he spoke of the need to look after wildlife to ensure its future. I absorbed every word.

Dale Hudson kept me busy most days. Although the work entailed physically demanding chores such as pulling stumps and hauling water, I was happy. The guests came from as far away as Florida and paid big bucks for the privilege. And here I was getting paid (nominally, I recall) to be there. Whenever I had some spare time, I'd go fishing.

Taking a break on a dock one afternoon, I cast out a floating popper-type lure that I'd never used before. I had jerk-retrieved it only four times when, suddenly, the popper disappeared in a big swirl. Ten minutes later, I landed a pike of about six pounds. I couldn't believe it. I couldn't figure out what food the pike had associated with the popper. A few days later, I had the answer.

Casting from the same dock, I spotted a hen mallard and six fist-sized yellow ducklings paddling toward me. As I briefly looked away, I heard a splash in the direction of the ducks. The water looked as if someone had thrown in a rock. The ducks – mother quacking, her ducklings peeping as they tried to keep up – were scooting off in obvious alarm. I was puzzled until I counted the ducklings: five. A pike had dined – and my mind made the popper connection.

Later, I told the story to Henry Bradley. "I've seen that happen many times," he said. "A pike doesn't turn down an easy lunch."

★ ★ ★

Sarah cast out her line and watched the slip-bobber settle on the calm water. Our boat was anchored off a rocky drop-off in a long, finger-shaped bay southwest of the camp. It was about 9 p.m., and we'd been fishing since 7:30. It was still light, with a full moon starting to faintly appear.

A few hours after arriving in camp, we started fishing for walleye. It felt good to be back at Elbow Lake after so many years. We tried drifting bottom bouncers and night crawlers imported from our backyard in Alberta and jigging lead-heads tipped with frozen minnows. But slip bobbers and minnows quickly became our favourite method, not only because we caught lots of fish, but also because it allowed us to relax and talk.

Sarah's bobber began twitching and then, in a wink, disappeared. She wrenched back to set the hook, and her graphite rod bent under the weight of a solid fish. A few seconds later, Sarah reeled in a foot-long yellow perch. The minnow that had fooled it protruded from its lips.

"That would be good for breakfast," I said.

"Please don't kill it," she admonished. "I'm going to let it go."

Whether fishing for trout in the foothills of southern Alberta or walleye and perch in a remote lake in northern Manitoba, Sarah's personal no-kill policy is firm. A few minutes later, I caught a walleye of just over a pound.

"Now, *that's* breakfast," I said.

"That's up to you," Sarah replied. "I'd put it back."

"You don't have to eat any," I said.

"Well, if you're going to kill it, I'll help eat it."

We fished until 10:30 that night. Just before we quit, Sarah's eyes suddenly widened and she sat upright.

"Did you hear that?" she asked.

"No," I said, silently cursing my hearing impairment. "What was it?"

"A wolf," Sarah said, smiling broadly. "I just heard my first wolf howl."

The magic didn't stop there. On two afternoons, we

watched from our screened-in porch as an otter fished off a weed bed just 75 yards away. Loons called eerily near our boat while we fished. Lightning flashed in distant – and, quite suddenly, not so distant – skies as we fished one evening. We played cards, read, talked, cooked pizza and ate meals in our porch while peering at the water, distant shoreline and ospreys and white pelicans flying past. Our conversation changed from typical father–daughter chatter to deeper, topical subjects. I felt our bond grow stronger, almost imperceptibly. It was apparent we both knew we were sharing an experience that could never be duplicated.

One morning, before Sarah was awake, I motored over to the cairn memorial. Bird droppings stained a bronze plaque mounted on a slab of quartz-flecked granite. I rubbed away most of the white splatters with a wet cloth, then stood back to read the inscription beneath a simple engraving of pine cones and needle branches: *Henry Bradley 1919–1982. Veteran Trapper and Outstanding Conservationist. Lived Harmoniously with Man and the Environment He Loved.*

I closed my eyes and said a silent prayer of thanks for a great man and mentor, who so long ago had helped me see past bitterness and anger into a natural world of wildness and beauty. Henry had died at just 63 – only 15 years older than my present age. I imagined him in a better place, but couldn't really picture one nicer than this.

The next afternoon, while a howling wind and high white-caps kept us shore-bound, Sarah and I decided to hike over to Henry's old cabin. He'd built it in 1965, after taking over the trapline of J. Brydon Ashdown, who used to own the camp that was now Big Four. Henry wanted a place separate from the fishing camp. Somehow the cabin had escaped the big forest fire of 1989.

Sarah and I fought our way through willow bushes, a swamp and clouds of mosquitoes before finally reaching the clearing where the shack stood. My initial impression from the boat was confirmed. Since Henry's death, the place had been badly neglected and abused by the trapper who'd taken it over.

A shaggy blanket of tall grass and weeds covered the ground. The five-by-seven-metre cabin was made of chipboard once painted white. But now the cabin's paint was faded, the unshingled roof sagging and warped. Peeking through the windows, we could see the two rooms were a mess, with garbage, old clothes and bedding strewn about. Scattered throughout the surrounding trees were about a dozen wooden dog sheds, reminding me of the huskies Henry used that winter I shared with him. Across the yard, a log shed that Henry had kept clean and orderly was cluttered with broken snowshoes, a battered boltless Lee-Enfield .303 rifle and rusted traps hanging from nails in the wall. A rusted bedspring leaned on the outside wall. Remnants of three snowmobiles were scattered about; a fourth looked marginally operational. A 20-horsepower outboard motor, its paint chipped, hung from a plank nailed between two trees. The fully extended start cord dangled limply.

Sarah glanced at me and said I looked disappointed.

"Did you think it would still look the same as it did?" she asked.

"I guess you always expect it to be the way it was," I replied.

"But that was almost 30 years ago, Dad," Sarah succinctly noted.

★ ★ ★

Four days after arriving, it was time for us to leave. The adventure wasn't over, but it was time for the last leg. I watched with some sadness as the Cessna 185 floatplane taxied in to the dock. I'd decided that Sarah's first flight in any kind of airplane would be in a four-seater prop plane in northern Manitoba.

After loading our luggage and me into the rear of the plane, pilot Bob Gladstone helped Sarah into the co-pilot's seat beside him. About two minutes later, the plane lifted off the water and I watched the camp until I couldn't see it. I felt elated, happy to have made the trip back, but especially glad Sarah had been there to share it.

Fearing she might be nervous on her first flight, I tapped her on the shoulder and asked how it was going. Sarah smiled widely, silver braces on her teeth gleaming brightly, and gave me a thumbs-up.

★ ★ ★

It didn't take long for the train chugging north from Cranberry

Portage to enter a frosty world of snow-blanketed trees and ice-entombed lakes.

It was January 1972, and I was on a slow train for the 40-kilometre trip to Heming Lake, a barren siding with a winter population of one old trapper who lived in a log cabin. I was en route to meet Henry Bradley, and as the train moved slowly along, I kept wondering whether he'd be there. With the temperature hovering at minus-35 and a ticket that only went as far as Heming Lake, I'd be in deep trouble if he weren't.

I'd graduated high school the previous June and was at loose ends. I'd come north by Greyhound from Winnipeg to Flin Flon, where I tried to get a job at a gold mine. Unsuccessful, I travelled 52 kilometres by bus back south to Cranberry Portage. Sitting in an old café, I considered my options: return to Winnipeg a 19-year-old failure and resume my job search, or try to reach Henry Bradley's cabin at Elbow Lake.

Problem was, the region was locked in winter's grip, and getting there would be difficult. Some locals ride in by snowmobile, a trip of several hours over the three frozen Cranberry lakes and the Grass River. Without a snowmobile, my only option was the train. Every two days, a Canadian National train ran north from the Pas to the mining town of Lynn Lake, depositing and picking up passengers at several Aboriginal settlements along the way. It returned every other day.

The local ticket agent told me my best bet would be to try to get word to Henry Bradley that I'd be at Heming Lake on a certain day. Then I'd have to hope he'd be there to greet me with

123

a snowmobile or his dogsled. With Heming Lake 13 miles west of Elbow Lake, and communications quite iffy, I knew it was a crapshoot. And in winter in the middle of nowhere, it was a highly risky crapshoot.

The only communication option was the local radio station. I knew Henry had a small transistor radio, but I didn't know if he ever listened to it. The radio station in Flin Flon had an evening call-in program that served as a kind of primitive call centre for residents of remote reserves and settlements. People would phone to tell relatives that they were getting out of hospital, that they had a new baby or that they were arriving in a few days for a visit. One night, I phoned the station and asked them to broadcast a message to Henry Bradley at Elbow Lake that Bruce – I didn't give my last name – would be arriving at Heming Lake two afternoons later.

I phoned home to Winnipeg and asked Dad to ship up my snowshoes, sleeping bag, .22 rifle and other essentials on the bus. Along with extra clothes and a few groceries, that's all I had with me on the train. As the train drew nearer to Heming Lake, I started worrying that Henry hadn't received the message. After a ride of about 90 minutes, the conductor walked by and announced "Next stop: Heming Lake." Looking out the window, I saw a frozen lake and not much else. I thought: I am nuts, absolutely nuts. But when the door opened, a tall man in heavy fur-trimmed parka stood on the snow below me. It was Henry. Behind him was a sled and team of nine Siberian huskies. Shouldering my duffel bag, I stepped down and shook his wool-mittened hand. "Oh, it's you," Henry said, smiling. "I didn't know which Bruce was coming to see me." After loading my gear onto the sled, I walked behind as Henry drove the dogs a few hundred yards to a log cabin. Inside, he introduced me to a grizzled old trapper named Joe. As Joe served tea, Henry explained how lucky I'd been.

"I almost never listen to that radio," he said. "I was sitting there reading my Bible and something made me turn it on. I just about fell out of my chair when I heard a message for me." Although bitterly cold, it wasn't snowing, so Henry decided to travel by dog team to meet his mystery visitor. Later, drifting off to sleep after a supper of boiled moose meat, I couldn't help but think that I must have a guardian angel.

The next morning, Henry hitched the dogs to their leather harnesses and we took off for Elbow Lake. I felt like a character in a Jack London novel. With me bundled in a blanket on the sled and Henry balanced on the wooden runners, the team travelled along narrow trails and over frozen lakes, the only sound the whoosh of the runners on the snowy ground. Overhanging pine boughs laden with clumps of fluffy snow dumped their loads down our necks as we brushed them while passing underneath. Going up hills, Henry and I both jumped off and pushed. After an hour, he declared it was time for me to mush. Henry sat on the sled and shouted commands to the dogs while I desperately grasped the wooden handles and tried to stay upright. Once, I slipped and tumbled off, then watched as the sled disappeared around a bend. Henry shouted whoa to stop the dogs. By the time I struggled through the thigh-deep snow to reach them, the team was under control.

Arriving at Henry's cabin at Elbow Lake was the start of an unforgettable five-week adventure.

He showed me how to set traps for lynx, wolf, mink, red squirrel, muskrat and beaver. Several times, he dispatched me to trek solo on snowshoes to check sets in the forest several kilometres away. I carried my .22 single-shot Cooey or Henry's over-under Savage combination 20-gauge/.22 and pretended I was a real trapper. My route took me through a frozen swamp. One day I encountered the tracks of several wolves that hadn't been there the day before. I spent the rest of the day nervously looking around me. Sometimes I'd shoot a snowshoe hare and bring it back for supper. Otherwise, we ate moose carved from a frozen carcass stored in a shed. One day I went to check the traps and they were empty. The next day, Henry returned from the same area and reported that he'd caught nothing but a track from a size-ten boot. Mine. I'd clumsily stepped on and obliviously triggered a leghold trap hidden by a dusting of light snow. I didn't even know about it until he told me. Henry was a master tracker, and eagerly taught this city kid about animal tracks and other sign. He pointed out the difference between moose and caribou tracks, and once showed me where a wolverine had loped on top of crusty snow. "I hope he stays away from my traps," Henry said. Once, he pointed at a snowbank three metres away and said, "Ptarmigan." I saw nothing. Then he told me to look for black eyes. When I did, I picked out six white ptarmigan huddled motionless against the snow.

Henry monitored populations of the animals he trapped as carefully as a rancher tends his cattle herd. He spoke often of the need to regulate his wild harvest. If he noticed lynx numbers were down, for example, he would stop setting for lynx for a season. Same with red squirrel, beaver and other species. At night, under the light of a propane lantern, he carefully skinned his catch, gently stroking the fur while he stretched the hides on boards. In the spring, he'd ship his fur to Winnipeg.

In those five weeks, Henry used his snowmobile sparingly, preferring to travel by dogsled. "You don't have to worry about the dogs breaking down or running out of gas," he explained. When they weren't working, the huskies were chained to steel stakes driven into the frozen ground. They slept curled up in tight balls, falling snow covering their thick coats until they were almost invisible. Henry allowed me to feed the dogs frozen whitefish, but cautioned me against getting too close. "A few have some wolf in them," he warned. After a few weeks, the quiet, rust-coloured lead dog, Red, seemed to warm to me. One day, as I reached to rub his head, he lunged at me with fangs bared. I jumped back. Watching us, Henry grinned and said, "Told ya."

In the evening, Henry and I sat at opposite ends of the kitchen table, the crackling wood stove warding off minus-40 temperatures outside. He seldom played the radio, something I contemplated a lot, considering the surprise nature of my visit. We played cribbage and talked, me of life in Winnipeg, Henry of his choice to live off the land. Smoking thin roll-your-owns, he sat quietly late at night, reading his worn Bible and sipping tea. I never saw him angry or befuddled. Henry seemed to be a man at peace with himself. As a confused 19-year-old with what I perceived as limited future prospects, I was envious.

One morning, Henry announced it was time to put up ice for the two fishing lodges on Elbow Lake. Each camp had a wood-framed ice house, which provided cold storage and a steady ice supply all summer. For four days, we chain-sawed heavy rect-angular blocks of ice from the frozen lake. After lifting them out with steel tongs, we used block and tackle to winch them ashore. The ice was stacked in the sheds, covered with layers of sawdust for insulation. It was hard, exhausting work. One time, I was pulling on the rope to move a block of ice toward the shore when suddenly the heavy steel anchor ripped out of the icehouse wall. It flew past me like a bullet, narrowly missing my head. I shook for several minutes, and once again had thoughts of a guardian angel.

Five wonderful weeks after the adventure began, it was time to head home, find a job, and decide what to do with my life. Henry needed supplies, so he decided to take me out by snow-mobile. We travelled along Elbow Lake, then southwest along the three Cranberry Lakes and the frozen Grass River, back-tracking the same route I'd taken by boat in the summer of '70. At one point, Henry stopped his machine and pointed across the lake at a small herd of woodland caribou running over the ice. A few minutes later, we saw the reason they were running: five *wolves loped along in the general direction of the caribou, without really seeming to be hunting them. Shortly after, Henry was driving the machine tight along the shoreline when suddenly we started sinking in slushy rotten ice. "Get off, it's a spring," he yelled with more urgency than I'd ever seen him show. As I leaped from the snowmobile and scrambled to shore, my pant legs were soaked right through. My heart pounded and I felt like I'd once again cheated death. Henry revved the snowmobile and it found solid ice. Fifty yards distant, he stopped so I could get back on. My pant legs froze solid within seconds.*

Finally, Cranberry Portage came into view. We pulled onto the shoreline near the dock on which I'd waited for a boat two summers ago. Later, as I climbed onto the Greyhound bus heading south, I vowed to return. I never imagined it would take almost 30 years – and that I'd never see him again.

★ ★ ★

The boxcar was a clutter of canoes, backpacks, tents, rod cases and beer coolers. Sarah and I were sharing the train car with four new friends from Flin Flon, carefree middle-aged men married to four singing sisters from the northern mining town. The men were on a stag canoeing/fishing/beer-guzzling trip to Heming Lake. Sarah and I were on a different kind of mission: a pilgrimage to a place I hadn't seen since January 1972.

Waiting for the train on a hot, sunny July afternoon was a sharp contrast to that frigid January day so many years earlier. Heat reflected off the steel rails as Sarah and I set down our packs crammed with tent, sleeping bags, fishing tackle, clothing, food and water. By the time the train arrived almost two hours late, we'd witnessed a veritable parade of northern humanity. Girls Sarah's age and younger carried newborn babies or showed obvious signs of pregnancy. About a dozen young men formed a circle behind the boarded-up train station and passed around a joint. A young man offered to sell me a Sony PlayStation, then enthusiastically admired the fancy camera hanging around my neck.

Eventually, we wandered to the other side of the station and met the four brothers-in-law. When the train finally pulled up, it didn't take much to convince us to travel with them in the boxcar with all our gear rather than in a crowded passenger car. So there we sat for almost one hour on the ride to Heming Lake. Concerned we might roast in the oven-like car, the crewmen had left the sliding door wide open, affording us a panoramic moving view of lakes, rocks and forests. We sat on cardboard boxes full of canned soup and on cases of disposable diapers. One guy found a chair for Sarah and there she sat, like a queen in her court, listening to our chatter. Five icy cans of beer appeared. We were riding in luxury.

When we finally stopped at Heming Lake, I felt a little morose. I knew Henry Bradley wouldn't be waiting to greet us, and old Joe the trapper would be long gone. And although we searched hard, Sarah and I couldn't even find his old cabin. It was like a piece of history had vanished.

Our friends stayed put to set up camp. Sarah and I opted to trudge north one mile, despite the oppressive heat. We needed to be close to the lake's only dock, where Bob Gladstone could pick us up in his Cessna the next afternoon. Eventually, Sarah found us an ideal camping spot in a mossy clearing surrounded by towering pines. As I stood contemplating the site, she asked if Heming Lake looked familiar. "Not really," I said. "But it was winter and a long time ago."

After hanging the food from a rope strung high between two trees, Sarah and I set up the tent and unrolled our sleeping bags. We ducked inside to escape hordes of hungry black flies. A cool breeze wafted through the screened windows while flies buzzed frantically outside. After a while, we ventured out, donned net hats and face covers and went to see the lake. The water was blue and expansive, quite unlike my first time here. In early evening, we cooked canned stew on a single burner stove and boiled water for hot chocolate. Before long, we retired to the tent to read and savour the silence. Sleep came quickly.

After breakfast, we explored the forest and walked along the lakeshore. When Sarah retired to the tent to escape the flies, I spent a few hours fishing, fooling several pike with hooks baited with night crawlers. Then it was time to pack up and head over to the dock. Bob Gladstone was on time. The 20-minute flight back to Cranberry Portage was bumpy. But Sarah, sitting in the co-pilot's spot, couldn't stop smiling.

Our northern adventure had come to a close. Sarah and I had shared an experience that neither one of us will forget. I'd dreamed for many years of returning to this destination of my youth, the home of Henry Bradley, a man who never went back to the land because he never left it. It took many years for me to realize it, but that special place and time had forever seared on my psyche a need to connect with wild places, to hunt and fish and explore, and to share that passion with others.

Together, Sarah and I had made a journey of the heart. Now that it was over, I felt a little sad, but at the same time blessed to have had the opportunity to do it with such a special person.

★ ★ ★

One peaceful evening at Elbow Lake, Sarah and I sat quietly in the screened veranda as sunset cast a rich golden hue over the still water. A loon's cry echoed eerily. I was lost in memories old and new. Suddenly, inspiration struck and I was surprised to hear myself say, "Maybe some day, I'll bring one of your kids here."

Turning to face me, Sarah smiled as she spoke.

"Maybe I'll come, too."

To this father, sweeter words could never be heard.

IN THE FIELD

A NATURAL BOND

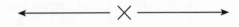

They were two very different conversations with two totally different people. But their words had a similar ring, and really got me thinking about this thing called hunting.

The first chat was with a newspaper reporter colleague whose opinion I respect. He doesn't hunt, but his father did.

Spotting an outdoor magazine lying on my desk, the reporter admired an artist's rendition of a wide-antlered whitetail buck standing in the snow that took up the entire front cover.

"I could never shoot that," my friend declared. "It looks so nice."

Smiling, I picked up the magazine so I could have a better look.

"Yes, it is lovely," I replied. "But I'd shoot it if I had the chance."

The second conversation happened the same week.

It was with an older friend, who had hunted for more than 50 years before hanging up his guns forever.

"I just couldn't do it anymore," he told me. "Pulling the trigger made me sick."

I told both of these friends that I respected their feelings. They'd made their own choices.

But I also exhorted them to respect hunters who choose to hunt, to participate in a legal activity steeped in tradition, all in the name of recreation and wildlife management.

"Why do you hunt?" my newspaper colleague asked, genuinely interested in my answer.

Every fall, for more than five decades, I have asked myself that question. The season I stop asking it will be the year I quit hunting.

Hunters have a responsibility to understand not only why they hunt but why other people don't. We must respect the opinions of non-hunters while at the same time standing firm in our own deep-rooted beliefs.

I started hunting as a teenager growing up in Winnipeg. After passing a firearms safety course, I would accompany my father on grouse-hunting excursions to a public forest east of the city. Those were cherished times, a chance for rare one-on-one time with the busy salesman, an experience child development experts later labelled "quality time."

Carrying first a .22-calibre Winchester Cooey Model 39 and later a single-shot 12-gauge shotgun – both guns purchased with money I earned delivering newspapers and painting fences – I spent many Saturdays tromping through the forest with my dad, in search of spruce and ruffed grouse. Some days we took home a few birds for supper. Some days we didn't. But it didn't matter.

What mattered was that we were out together, exploring the woods, seeing deer and other wildlife, sharing a stump while munching our sandwiches and requisite Eat-More chocolate bars. Dad and I had an uneasy relationship at home, but I felt like we were true friends when we were afield together. We talked about major issues of the day, work and life itself. Shooting birds was of secondary importance.

Conservation writer Kevin Van Tighem addresses this phenomenon in his book *Coming West: A Natural History of Home*:

> As any hunter knows, a dead thing does not a successful hunt make, any more than an empty freezer equals a wasted fall. Sometimes we ourselves forget what those who do not hunt cannot understand: That it is not merely the kill that makes us hunters.
>
> It is the witnessing, the being there, and those intimate moments of belonging when the living world reveals itself to those who work so hard to become a part of it. We are not seeking death. We are actively participating in, and celebrating, the incredible richness of life.

Van Tighem knows better than most about the finite relationship between wildlife, its habitat, people and where we choose to live, and how sometimes we cause that relationship to be compromised.

To some non-hunters, and certainly to ardent anti-hunters,

being a hunter, conservationist, ecologist and naturalist is a contradiction in terms. But that attitude has been shown to be misguided by the efforts of respected and influential North American hunter/naturalists, including Van Tighem; Canadian conservation scholar Ian McTaggart-Cowan; Aldo Leopold, considered the father of ecology; William Dutcher, founder of the National Audubon Society; and US president Teddy Roosevelt, who created the model for our continent's national park system and wildlife refuges.

People are natural predators, plain and simple. Many of us eat meat and some of us don't. But we all eat food bought in supermarkets or grown in gardens. Some people choose to suppress their predatory instincts. They allow others to do their killing so they can buy food nicely wrapped and packaged and keep their own hands free of the blood involved in the process. Hunters choose to gather their own healthy and organic wild meat, while at the same time enjoying spectacular sunrises, seeing wildlife and touching the land. Our family gets to eat wild game – venison, upland birds and waterfowl – that I've shot. Karen eats it, our daughters were raised on it and I get satisfaction from being a hunter/gatherer.

Ethical and responsible hunters also care deeply about maintaining a balance of wildlife – game and non-game species alike – and ardently defend the environment in which birds and animals live.

Our physical and spiritual connection with wild things

and wild places helps shape who we are and how we look at life.

Hunting is not for everyone, nor should it be. But for those of us who hunt, it is a way of life. Our life.

AWAKENING THE SENSES

The snow was new and soft, a natural welcome mat at the foot of the ridge. Somewhere, a raven delivered a guttural greeting to the autumn sun easing over the ridge to the east. Another raven answered.

Tracks in the snow told the story of a couple of coyotes passing this way not many hours earlier. Their paths, leading from one willow clump to another, suggested they were hunting for a vole or rabbit, maybe a grouse.

My heart quickened when I cut the trail of a moose, dew claws leaving small imprints in the snow behind saucer-sized cloven hooves. A big animal, I thought; probably a bull. It was opening day of hunting season, and I had moose and mule deer tags in my pocket.

Hoping to spot the beast feeding placidly on willows flanking the beaver-dam-etched swamp ahead, I moved silently through the trees, carefully placing each heavily booted foot to avoid snapping a twig. In the cool air, my breath puffed smoke-like from mouth and nostrils.

The track threaded through the trees, hoofprints clear and even-paced, suggesting this was a moose on a mission but not yet aware it was being followed. Finally, realizing I wasn't going to see the moose on its own level, I stepped onto a narrow game trail leading up the ridge.

I hoped higher elevation would provide me an advantage, a glimpse of the moose without it knowing I was there. The daypack heavy on my back, I stopped several times to admire the view, providing an opportunity to catch my breath while carefully scanning the trees below me for the moose.

The tree-lined trail was a veritable coyote highway. Tracks of several coyotes heading up and down the ridge intersected with coyote prints heading north and south along the side hill. In a few places, tiny pairs of dots clearly showed atop the coyote tracks. In nature's supreme irony, mice had opted to travel on the snow packed hard by the very predators that were hunting them.

As I climbed the ridge, my mind wandered back to an earlier autumn at the same place. That was the morning I spotted four-toed cougar tracks that appeared to have been made the night before. Each print was a broad, bell-shaped main pad behind four oval toe prints, claws retracted like that of a house cat. The cat was heading south, weaving through the poplars, black spruce and willow, where mule deer and snowshoe hares hung out.

Silently, I cheered the cougar's survival in a region increasingly dotted by acreages often occupied by people who often don't realize the impact their chosen lifestyle has on the local wildlife. I hoped against hope to see the cat. I never did.

Forcing my mind back to the day at hand, I resumed my hike up the ridge, ever hopeful that today might yield another cougar track. As I topped the ridge, which was painted with greens and yellows of changing leaves against a snow-white backdrop, I peered over the other side. A creek bravely trickled down the valley. In a few weeks, it would be frozen solid.

By now, the sun had vanished behind the clouds, and the lead-grey sky threatened snow. I deeply inhaled fresh, crisp air.

Leaning against a poplar tree, I peered through the binoculars at open meadows pocking the heavily treed ridge facing me. I meticulously dissected the landscape, searching for an out-of-place horizontal line in the trees that might betray the presence of a bedded mule deer buck. Nothing. I shouldered the pack and continued along the trail.

Occasionally changing my route to cut over to the edge on either side and peer down at the valleys flanking the ridge, I searched for deer, moose, elk, coyote – in fact, anything other than the Hereford cows that dotted the landscape in every direction. I knew mule deer lived here. I'd seen them many times before. For more than an hour, I walked the ridge top without spotting any wildlife.

Then, just when I was about to give up and abandon the ridge for the valley below, there they were: fresh tracks of a half dozen mule deer crossing the narrow trail from east to west. One track was exceptionally broad and heavy. Maybe a buck.

All senses now on full alert, I started following the tracks slowly and deliberately. I stayed on the trail for several hundred yards, stopping often to train the binoculars on the terrain ahead in case the deer were bedded down and watching their back-trail, as they are wont to do.

But the deer continued to elude me. Tired, and knowing I had a long walk back, I finally gave up and dropped down into the valley, where I found a main trail. Two hours later, I was back at my vehicle.

As I unloaded the rifle and slid it back into its case, I gave silent thanks for the day, and also for the fact that I hadn't seen any game.

After all, hunting season is too special to end it the first day out.

PASSING THE BUCK

It was a perfect fall morning, one of those special times you just know something is going to happen. A foot of snow had fallen the night before, creating ideal conditions for still-hunting a poplar forest at the foot of the Rockies. I'd covered maybe a quarter mile when, suddenly, my attention was drawn to a horizontal shape about 100 yards away.

Scanning with the binoculars, I could see it was a downed poplar. But my heart quickened when I soon realized what was behind it: a bedded whitetail buck. And not just any old run-of-the-mill buck. With each side sporting five heavy and high tines, the rack extended well past its ears. It was the largest buck I'd ever had a chance to shoot.

The deer peered intently in my direction, seemingly unsure what I was. Decked out head to toe in snow-pattern camouflage, I blended perfectly with the terrain. I leaned against a tree and watched the deer watching me. The dead poplar lay diagonally across the buck's chest, leaving only the white throat patch exposed. I slowly put the crosshairs on that patch, cranked the scope to eight power and considered taking the shot. But I wasn't sure I could kill the deer cleanly in its bed. I'd heard horror stories about deer running around with their jaws shot off, the result of poorly placed neck or head shots, eventually succumbing to a slow and painful death from starvation. I was determined this great deer would be taken quickly and cleanly, or not at all.

For several long minutes, I willed the deer to stand and present a broadside shot. My heart raced. My hands started trembling, and not from the cold. It was a waiting game, I knew, but I was becoming impatient. I edged slightly to my right. At the movement, the buck instantly stood, presenting a quartering away view. Its coat was distinctively rust-coloured in the sunshine. I squeezed the trigger and the shot shattered the silence. The buck jumped straight up, turned and vanished in the trees. I leaned against a tree and took a deep breath. The shot had seemed good. I was sure the buck was piled up nearby. I covered the 100 yards quickly. As I searched the fresh snow, however, I couldn't find any blood or hair. My heart sank.

Finally, I glimpsed a clump of thick hair hanging from a willow several feet away. It was a patch of guard hair from along the buck's back. I silently cursed myself for shooting too high, for somehow managing to shave off the hair while completely missing the spine. Seeing no blood anywhere, I began to follow the trail. At first, the buck appeared to be bounding along. Then it slowed to a walk. When the tracks reached a frozen creek, the deer jumped it, without showing any sign of being wounded.

After going several hundred yards without seeing any blood, I started backtracking. I'd gone about 100 yards when I froze. A drop of blood, no larger than a pencil eraser, dotted the snow beside the track. I couldn't believe I'd missed seeing it the first time past. Several feet later, I saw another blood drop, then another in the deer's track. I eventually saw six tiny drops of blood. At that point, my attitude changed drastically. The deer was wounded. It wasn't hit solidly, to be sure, but it was definitely hit. Returning to the creek, I decided to give the buck a chance to bed down and, hopefully, die. Sitting on a log, I forced myself to wait 30 minutes, beating myself up repeatedly over my shoddy marksmanship. However, for the first time since pulling the trigger, I started thinking that just maybe I'd be putting my tag on this dream buck. I resumed tracking, encouraged by single fresh blood spots every 50 to 100 yards.

The buck led me to a thick patch of willows, which it circled three times. Twice, I found the deer's deep hoofprints where it had stepped in my own boot tracks. Finally, the buck left the willows and started heading toward a low ridge. I moved slowly and silently. After several hundred yards, I saw the ridge through the trees. I stopped to scan the thin edge of forest separating me from the foot of the ridge. A rusty patch slowly materialized in the trees just 50 yards away. A deer. But was it the buck?

Willows and a big poplar tree shielded the animal's head. All I could see was the body and distinctive tail of a whitetail. It was on the same trail of the track I was following. It was a large-bodied deer, but I wasn't sure it was a buck.

Although it had the same reddish coat of the buck I'd shot at, I couldn't swear it was the same animal. I could tell by the deer's posture that it was looking backwards at me. I had a clear shot at its heart and lungs. I struggled with my options. If indeed it was *the* buck, I could kill it cleanly right now and take satisfaction that I'd hunted well – at least after the initial rushed shot. I recalled the buck's wide, thick rack when I'd first seen it. I pictured that head on my office wall and its flesh in the freezer, providing a year's supply of meat for my family and a lifetime's supply of memories and stories I could embellish with each telling.

Without moving my body, I strained to see the spot where I judged the deer's head to be. I was desperate for even just a glimpse of antler tine. Without that crucial confirmation, however, shooting this deer wasn't even an option. Although I was 99.9 per cent certain this was the buck I was after, what if it was a big doe? Doe season wasn't open. What if I shot and then discovered I'd made a mistake?

What would I do then? Walk away and pretend it hadn't happened? Turn myself in? So many questions. But there was only one answer: don't shoot, you idiot. I subscribe to and preach the gospel of hunting responsibly, ethically and within the law. My vehicle bears a Report-A-Poacher licence plate. Shooting without being absolutely 100 per cent sure of my target was out of the question.

The deer didn't move a hair. The standoff couldn't have lasted five minutes, but it seemed like hours. Once again, I decided to try to make something happen. If I could move just a few inches, I reasoned, I might see at least a portion of the rack. Presented with even a hint of antler, I would shoot. At my slight movement, the deer reacted as if poked with an electric cattle prod. As it bolted from the trees, the first thing I noticed was the huge set of antlers. The second thing was that it didn't appear to be hurt in any way. Quartering away and shielded by trees and brush, the buck ascended the ridge in a few seconds flat. I had no clear shot.

But it was heading for an open notch in the trees about 75 yards away. I raised my rifle and waited. The buck was closing fast. Fifty yards, 40 yards, 20, 10. I slipped off the safety and took a deep breath. But then I watched, incredulously and helplessly, as the buck veered right just inches before reaching the clearing.

In a heartbeat, the deer disappeared into the trees. Slumping against a tree, I felt drained, emotionally and physically. I was wracked by disappointment and self-doubt. I knew that, by now, the buck likely would have cleared the four-strand barbed wire fence separating the top of the ridge from the neighbouring private property. A few days earlier, the landowner had rather curtly denied me access permission. He'd actually laughed as his blue heeler cattle dog nipped the seat of my pants as I returned to my vehicle.

I briefly considered approaching the same rancher, appealing for permission to track the wounded buck. But could I say, with any real conviction, that the buck was mortally – or even seriously – wounded? It had easily jumped a six-foot creek. It had effortlessly ascended a steep ridge without any sign of being wounded. It never bedded down after that first shot. The blood spots were tiny and infrequent. I decided my bullet had merely clipped the hair on its back, just nicking the hide and flesh with a wound that would heal in a day or two. If I couldn't convince myself this deer was wounded, no way would I convince the landowner to allow me on his property to try and track it.

I've relived that experience in my head countless times. As I rewind it, fast-forward it and play it through, I can't think of anything I could have done better, or differently – except for being more careful with that first shot. Every buck I see reminds me of that big-racked foothills ghost. I've never had a shot at another buck like that one. Perhaps I never will.

That deer taught me a thing or two about hunting. But the important lesson was the one it taught me about myself.

CARL'S KNIFE

It's funny how a simple, inanimate object like an old hunting knife can bring into sharp focus the abstract meanderings of the human mind. But that it did, last week, while I was peacefully hiking along a ridge top in search of cow elk.

It had been a frustrating elk season. Mild temperatures coupled with no snow and ripping warm Chinook winds had combined to sabotage many elk-hunting expeditions. Early in the season, a fair number of elk fell to hunters' guns.

But then the going got tough. Forest floors were covered with a blanket of dry leaves and deadfall that rustled loudly when stepped upon, announcing hunters' presence to all wildlife in the vicinity. The elk stayed up high in the mountains, munching on tall grass left bare by unseasonably warm weather. While the rest of the world welcomed the nice weather, foothills elk hunters cursed it and prayed for snow and cold.

Many cow elk permit holders, myself included, sat back smugly, knowing that we had an extra two weeks to hunt after the general bull elk, moose and deer season had ended. However, the warm weather continued into the extended season, and hunters were spotting few elk.

On the last day of the extended season, I was hunting an area that traditionally had held elk – at least during seasons when the weather cooperated. But on this day there was not even a promising-looking track of any kind to be found, much less that of a cow elk.

Somehow, though, I didn't feel disappointed.

For the first morning in several weeks, the wind wasn't howling like a banshee through the woods. A welcome snowfall – albeit too little, too late – had carpeted the forest floor, muffling my footsteps as I hunted. Fresh snowflakes sprinkled my coat.

Under these long-awaited perfect conditions, my senses should have been focused on hunting. Instead, they felt dulled, possibly from too many miles and too many days spent without even seeing an elk.

Rather than thinking about elk, I found my thoughts drifting to why I hunt, the intangible factors that transcend filling the freezer and the enjoyment of being outdoors. That's when I remembered the knife.

It had been given to me three months earlier during a pre-season visit from an elderly neighbour, a retired oil rig worker who had hunted all his life until, several years earlier, age and a bad ankle had forced him to quit. But Carl still likes to swap hunting tales and has been known to accept a venison roast.

A few days before deer season opened, I answered a rap on my front door to find my white-haired neighbour standing there. He said nothing as he reached into his coat pocket and brought out a knife.

"I want you to have this," he said. "I'll never use it again."

My spine tingled as he handed me the knife encased in a beautifully crafted, home-cut leather sheath. Just before I could take it in hand, Carl hesitated. For just a second or two, he held it back, possibly reflecting that with the knife he was giving up a big part of himself and an activity he had loved.

As knives go, it wouldn't stand out in a crowd. The handle was made of bone, faded and rubbed smooth from many decades of use. The blade was scalpel-sharp, but longer and more pointed than what I like in a knife used for skinning and field-dressing game animals. Carl had owned the knife since 1929, and age had erased all but a few letters of the Swedish manufacturer's name from the blade. His wife, Mary, had cut the leather and hand-stitched the sheath.

I knew the knife was worth much more than its mere monetary value. It shone with proud tradition and hard use. It reflected many hunting seasons and animals taken to feed Mary and Carl. A priceless legacy had been handed down from one generation to another.

After we shook hands, Carl declined my offer of coffee. Then he turned and walked away in silence.

As I stood in the woods in a light snowfall several weeks later, I removed Carl's knife from the sheath strapped to my belt. I turned it over carefully in my hand, admiring how at different angles the blade showed varying hues of blue. In its first season with me, I'd used the knife to skin and dress two deer. It had already served me well.

But its real function was much more than utilitarian. It had helped me carry on Carl's hunting tradition. It represented his past and my future in the field. It helped reinforce in me that while we should strive to preserve wildlife and hunting for future generations, we also need to preserve hunting in honour of those like Carl who have gone before.

I slipped the knife back into the sheath. After pulling the coat's snow-flecked collar up around my neck, I quietly walked out of the forest and drove home for the last time that season, leaving one more cow elk to live another year, hopefully to produce another generation.

Thanks, Carl.

BELLE

———————— × ————————

Belle sits at the ready, eyes ablaze with anticipation as she peers skyward waiting for the October morning magic to begin. And when it happens, when that first green-winged teal suddenly jets in from the east, directly out of the glaring blind spot caused by the bright sun topping the pumpkin-orange horizon, Belle spots it first and makes the announcement with a frantic wagging of her tail.

Although I anticipated this moment, planned for it, and should have been ready, somehow I'm still surprised to see the bird. I quickly stand up from my willow bush blind, raise the shotgun, and then immediately lower it when I realize the duck is long gone.

Expecting the shot, Belle had jumped up, all four legs ramrod-stiff under a black body quivering with excitement. When the shotgun remains silent, she turns around and her soft brown eyes peer at me curiously, without a hint of judgement or accusation. That look – which every dog-owning hunter knows – personifies the special and timeless relationship between hunter and hunting dog, a relationship built on trust and mutual admiration. It's a look that says, "I won't expect perfection from you if you don't expect it from me."

But, most of all, it's a look of love.

Pennsylvania author Charles Fergus explores that relationship with poignant clarity in his delightful book *A Rough-Shooting Dog*. He says, "It is love (and of this I have no doubt) that makes a dog work the hardest for its master."

Hunters of waterfowl and upland birds share a special bond with their dogs, from flushers to pointers and everything in between. Anyone who has hunted with a good bird dog can't imagine going afield without one. For those hunters, chasing birds with a well-trained dog reduces the number of crippled or lost birds and maximizes the humane and ethical retrieval of downed birds.

However, more than just hunting efficiency is at stake here. A dogless hunter doesn't know the thrill of watching a dog work cover or swim out to retrieve a duck and then bring it back to you, while expecting no greater reward than a head pat and a whispered "Good girl (or boy)."

Without a dog, you're merely out walking with a shotgun, hoping the birds are where you think they should be, that you will be able to put them up and that they will land dead where they can be easily found by sight alone. And as any hunter of waterfowl or upland birds knows, that is a dream scenario, with little resemblance to reality.

★ ★ ★

"To arrive too early in the marsh is an adventure in pure listening; the ear roams at will among the noises of the night, without let or hindrance from hand or eye."

So wrote Aldo Leopold in his 1949 book *A Sand County Almanac*. Leopold's words clearly referenced human – not canine – senses. In the mysterious pre-dawn world, hunting dogs become complex four-legged radar screens of olfactory and visual signals, their senses further heightened by the occasional sound of a splash, har-onk of a goose or quack of a duck. On full alert in blind or boat, they never stop sniffing, cocking an ear to listen or trying to see through the darkness to identify all that they know, by instinct, is happening out there.

But things really get interesting for hunters and their dogs when the sun finally peeks over the horizon. For my own Belle, a Lab-golden retriever cross, that's the time to get down to the business at hand. It's when the birds fly, the master shoots and sometimes there's a goose or duck to retrieve. But it's also the time when, between action, musk-rats swim among our decoys, relentlessly teasing Belle by wiggling their little hairless rat-tails as they approach closer and closer.

For Belle, it can be just too much. Frequently, she has watched a muskrat so intently that she's becomes a veri-table mass of quivering nerves, with release coming only by jumping in the water in an attempt to catch it. These episodes always end with me yelling at her to get back in the boat or blind, and her scrambling back looking a little sheepish. The muskrat always escapes unscathed.

It's an indiscretion that some dog owners would never

forgive and would work hard to correct. I don't exactly approve, but somehow I can't get too upset when she does it. Like any relationship, ours involves give and take. I forgive Belle's odd behavioural lapse, and she forgives me when I fail by missing a bird or choosing the wrong place to hunt, which means a place devoid of game. Belle is not a perfect hunting dog, nor am I a perfect hunter. We've had almost 14 years to reach this understanding, and I don't regret a day of it. She's the best hunting dog our family has ever had.

Belle came into our life as a puppy, a product of a midnight country liaison between a purebred golden retriever female and a big black Lab that lived down the gravel road. The farm couple that owned the bitch was so upset at this unplanned breeding that they were giving away any puppy they could and planned to destroy the rest. When I went to see the litter (totally unbeknownst to Karen and our daughters – that's a story left for another day), five puppies scurried around on the ground below me. Belle was the only one that came up and nuzzled me. I was smitten, and later that afternoon she came home with me to meet the rest of the very surprised family.

Belle is a natural hunter. That isn't surprising considering her lineage. She was relatively easy to train to hand and whistle signals, and learned to follow my commands. When she was three months old, I was watching a hunting program on television one afternoon as Belle lay on the carpet. Suddenly, a cock pheasant angrily cackled on the screen as it was flushed. Belle immediately jumped up. Tail wagging, she ran to the television and pressed her nose to it. Naturally, I beamed proudly and enthusiastically praised her no end.

Displaying the best qualities of her parents as she developed, she took to hunting pheasant and partridge as eagerly as she did waterfowl over water and land. Belle finds wounded birds more efficiently than any dog I've ever known, pointers and flushers alike. Her spirit is unyielding in any weather and terrain.

We've hunted together in Montana, all over southern Alberta and, when she was 10, we flew to southern Ontario to hunt wood ducks and ruffed grouse with my cousin's husband. Last year, she made her final retrieve on her final hunt, although I didn't know at the time it would be.

We were hunting ducks on a late-October morning, on a spring-fed, fog-shrouded creek not far from our home. A dozen mallard decoys floated in front of our blind in the willows, which were thickly coated with white hoarfrost. Another half dozen standing decoys were stuck in the frozen mud along the shore.

We sat patiently for two hours, waiting for ducks to fly, but they never did. I didn't really mind – at least not for myself – because we'd already had several successful outings that season. But I was hoping for a duck, for Belle's sake. She sat patiently in the blind, shivering in the cold air and scanning the sky above for any sign of life.

Finally, the cold got to her and she started to whine. I decided we'd go for a walk, hoping to jump any ducks that might be hiding in the cattails and bulrushes along the creek. Minutes later, Belle suddenly started getting birdy. Her tail was wagging furiously as she plunged headlong into a thick cattail patch. A big cock pheasant exploded from the cover and presented an easy going-away shot.

The dead bird landed in the creek, and Belle was on it instantly, hitting the water with a splash and swimming strongly toward it until she clenched it in her jaws. Seconds later she handed the rooster to me, getting the mandatory head rub in return. It was our last bird of the season.

Four months later, the veterinarian diagnosed Belle with a heart condition. Later, she developed fluid in her lungs. Enjoy her during the summer, the vet advised, because she probably won't see much of the fall. Privately, I hoped that she'd at least make her 14th birthday on October 1.

Last week, Belle collapsed during a short walk not far from our house. I carried her back to a shaded grassy spot and laid her down. She lay flat on her side, eyes closed and chest heaving. I feared the worst. After 15 long minutes, Belle jumped to her feet and wagged her tail. At the vet's office, she was lethargic but her eyes looked perkier. The doc prescribed new heart medication and we headed home.

Belle has been sleeping a lot since then. The other night, she brought the ball to Karen and me and dropped it for us to throw, which we did. We know Belle doesn't have many days left. I only hope the end is painless – at least for her, because I know it won't be for us.

But when the end does come, I know our special relationship will never die. It will be preserved in a lifetime of memories of memorable hunts and not-so-memorable muskrats.

Every hunter should be so lucky.

HEARING VOICES

The bull elk was massive, with a huge, pulse-quickening set of antlers the likes of which I'd never seen outside a national park.

When I first saw it, the bull was hobbling along a barbed wire fenceline 200 yards away. A hind leg dragged uselessly behind in snow three feet deep. Then the elk stopped walking and casually peered in my direction.

As I stared at the bull, he stared back at me. Leaning against a fence post bordering a snow-blanketed pasture, I was wearing white-and-brown-splotched camouflage fleece pants and jacket, and a white wool toque to ward off the minus-22 chill on that late-November morning. My loaded .30-06 rifle was slung over my right shoulder.

The bull seemed to be trying to interpret this mysterious-looking lump in a place where he'd never seen one before. As he was trying to figure out what I was, I was fighting to decide whether to shoot him.

It shouldn't have been a difficult decision. Any other time it wouldn't have been. After all, it was 30 minutes into legal shooting time. The bull was on property I had permission to hunt, and I had a permit in my pocket. With my rifle sighted in to shoot an inch high at 200 yards, it would be a relatively easy shot, especially with the fence post for a steady rest.

And did I mention the size of the bull's antlers? Its beams were wide and heavy, with long, sweeping walnut-coloured tines polished white at the ends. I counted seven points on one side, six on the other. When the bull tipped his head back to sniff the crisp air, the antler tips grazed its yellowish butt patch. The body was massive, more Hereford than elk. It would provide a full year's worth of protein in the freezer.

More urgently, however, the bull was hurt. Its leg hung limply. I couldn't tell the cause of the injury. There was no blood. But I was certain that this mighty monarch was so badly wounded that it faced certain death from wolf or cougar in this heavily forested patch of foothills.

My mind raced as I factored each part of the equation. I was less than a mile from my vehicle, most of it downhill. I would have to quarter the bull to move it, but the sturdy plastic sled in the back of my van would make the hauling relatively easy. But wait. I was getting ahead of myself. There was a hitch, a really big hitch.

Just 15 minutes earlier, I'd pulled the trigger on a bull elk standing broadside in the field in front of me. But I didn't know if it was down, and I had a nagging feeling that the elk now looking at me might be the one I'd shot at.

It had all happened so fast ...

I'd parked my vehicle near the ranch buildings, cursing myself for arriving about ten minutes later than planned.

Hunting solo, I started snaking through the trees, heading toward the fenced pasture. Its far edge 600 yards away marked the boundary between the private land I was on and a large tract of public land.

I was planning to quickly cross the field and hunt for a whitetail buck on the public land. Although an elk tag was in my pocket, it was more of a secondary consideration, since over the years I'd seen very few elk in that field. An elk was the last thing on my mind. But as I quietly approached the edge of the poplars ringing the pasture, trying not to crunch the snow with my heavy boots, my plans suddenly changed, as plans often do when hunting. First one, then two, and then a third bull elk bolted from behind a brush pile and ran out into the open field. I leaned against a tree, pulled out my binoculars from under my coat, and started counting points.

The first bull was a spike, a year away from being legal in this zone, where bull elk must have at least three antler points on one side to be fair game. The second was a rag-horn four-point, a shooter by the regulations. But the third bull really set my heart a-thumping. It was farthest out in the pasture, standing broadside at just over 200 yards. Its antlers had more tines and looked heavier than the four-pointer. It was the largest bull I'd ever had in my scope. I stopped counting points once I determined it was legal.

Leaning against a poplar, I settled the crosshairs on the bull's barrel chest, just behind the front leg, and sent a

165-grain bullet on its way. At the shot, all three elk took off trotting across the field. The biggest one showed no sign of being hit. The two smaller ones ran directly toward the public land, jumped the fence and were gone. The big bull split off and wandered downhill toward a willow draw on the property I was hunting. By this time, he was too far and moving too fast for a second shot.

Hunters can be a funny lot. We anticipate that moment when a game animal suddenly appears before us. And then, when the animal doesn't immediately drop at the shot, we second-guess ourselves silly. That's exactly what happened as I watched the elk disappear in the willows.

Did I somehow miss completely? Did buck fever – bull fever? – take over my senses? Or did my bullet puncture the lungs as intended and now he's a dead elk walking? Have I wounded him? Will he escape into heavier cover?

Anxious for the answers, but keenly aware I shouldn't rush it, I decided to give the bull a full half-hour before I followed. I didn't want to push it into heavy timber, especially into the public no-man's land just a few hundred yards to the north. Perhaps it would give me another shot. Maybe, just maybe, I wouldn't need one.

All was quiet for several minutes as I waited by the fence, eyes riveted on the willow draw. The self-doubt gnawed at me. I worried the elk would move out the other end of the willow patch and into the forest. I'm not sure what made me look toward the east, but something did. When I slowly turned my head, I saw the monster bull hobbling along the fenceline marking the east end of the pasture.

At first it didn't seem likely that the bull I shot at could have come out of the willows in that direction without my noticing. I watched the bull for a few seconds, then peered back at the willow draw. Still nothing visible there. Suddenly I had sneaking suspicion that maybe this *was* the bull I'd shot at. The antlers on this bull looked larger than the one I'd shot at, but I hadn't really studied it before I fired. Maybe my scope was off and I'd hit the leg instead of the lungs. Maybe he'd sneaked out of the willows and was doing an end-run around me.

As indecision gripped my entire being, two conflicting invisible forces took over, whispering into my ears from opposite shoulders.

One said, "It's probably the bull you shot, and it's about to escape. And even if it is a second bull, it's obviously hurt and will die anyway. SHOOT IT!"

That voice turned distinctly devilish. "If it turns out you've killed the first bull, you can always find another hunter to tag it while you put your tag on this big guy. Or you can just leave the first one if it's dead. Its carcass will be gone by spring. Predators will pick it clean. You are now looking at a huge bull, buddy, bigger than you could ever hope for. And besides, maybe you completely missed that first bull and it has already sneaked out of the draw into the forest. You're getting a second chance here, you idiot. Take it!"

On the other shoulder perched a miniature angel that sounded a lot like my regular hunting partner, the most ethical and responsible hunter I've ever known.

"Hold on there," the angel whispered. "You had a solid rest on that first bull and you made a good shot. The bull separated from his buddies, always a good sign. He was hit hard. He's down in the willows. You're doing the right thing by waiting him out. Can you really live with yourself if you end up killing two elk this morning, with one of them being illegal? Do you really want to break the law? Do you really want to be a poacher?"

The moral tennis match played on in my mind a few more agonizingly long minutes. The huge bull continued limping along the fenceline. Twice it stopped to jump the fence and twice it aborted the attempt because of the injured leg. By the time the elk reached the final opening before entering the forest, I'd made my decision.

After sliding a cartridge into the chamber and nudging on the safety, I shouldered my rifle and slipped through the fence, creeping toward the willow draw where I hoped to find the bull I'd shot at. Thirty minutes had elapsed since I pulled the trigger.

My heart pounded harder with each step in the thigh-high snow. I easily picked up the bull's tracks, but started worrying when I couldn't spot even a single drop of blood. It was 150 yards to the edge of the willows. There was no elk, dead or alive, in sight. A jolt of self-doubt hit me like lightning.

After cresting a low rise, I saw where the bull had entered the willow patch, but I couldn't see any tracks leaving it. I slowly moved a few feet to the left to give myself a clearer view. There was the elk, just 75 yards away, lying dead in a small clearing with its legs folded under its tan-coloured body as if it was resting. As I reached in my pocket for the tag, I marveled at the bull's antlers – six long and heavy points to the side, rising high above the snow.

I gave thanks for the bull on the ground and the other bull that had limped into the forest, and for having the wisdom to make the right decision.

Two mornings later, I returned without my rifle to track the fenceline bull. A short distance into the forest, I was surprised to discover a long series of four distinct hoof-prints, with no trace of a dragging leg. In two places, he'd jumped fences without leaving even a hair on the barbs. Had he merely had some kind of temporary paralysis? A dislocated hip that somehow slipped back into place? I'll never know.

I never saw that elk again.

THE EMBARRASSING TRUTH

Aldo Leopold died more than half a century ago, but his words ring as true today as when they were first penned in the early 1900s. About hunting, the man who wrote the book on scientific wildlife management noted: "The hunter ordinarily has no gallery to applaud or disapprove his conduct. Whatever his acts, they are dictated by his own conscience rather than by a mob of onlookers."

He was referring to hunting ethics, or how hunters behave when no one is looking. Last fall, I had reason to wistfully contemplate those words as I lay sprawled flat on my back in an aluminum boat, staring up at the grey sky and feeling grateful I was alone.

Only seconds earlier I'd been securely perched on the middle seat of the boat, tucked snugly in a thick patch of bulrushes. I scanned the sky for ducks and geese while Belle sat on the stern seat, eagerly waiting for the action to begin.

Then a duck landed with a splash 200 metres away. Belle instantly leaped overboard and started swimming toward the bird. I blew the whistle and called in my sternest tone, but she totally ignored me. Suddenly two mallards appeared out of nowhere. I shot at the lead bird as it hit the one o'clock position. The second duck was directly above me when I fired the second barrel. Both shots missed, and the momentum of swinging the shotgun carried me past my centre of balance.

I fell backwards, landing heavily on the boat floor amid a jumble of decoy bags, oars, life jackets, lunch, gear and extra clothes. Stunned at my ineptitude, I stayed there for what seemed an eternity, occasionally uttering a half-hearted "Belle, come back here," before clumsily regaining my seat. Belle eventually returned, tired, cold and duckless. I nervously peered around to check for witnesses. Whew, I thought, greatly relieved – no mob of onlookers here.

Thankfully, the mob was likewise absent on another autumn morning when Belle and I set out in the boat in a pre-dawn fog thick enough to chew. Normally I would use the light in the farmyard across the lake as a guiding beacon to our bulrush blind, but on this morning I couldn't see it for the fog. Finally, after more than half an hour of vigorous rowing, the shoreline appeared, ghost-like, through the mist.

My heart sank as a parked van slowly came into view. Darn, I thought, some other hunter has jeopardized our morning hunt. But after focusing my binoculars on the vehicle, I sheeplishly realized it was mine. Disoriented in the fog, I had rowed full circle.

Again, we set off for the far shore. This time I strived to

put equal pressure on each oar to ensure the boat steered straight. The only sounds came from the creaking oarlocks, unseen ducks whistling by and Belle's tail thumping against the aluminum bow seat.

After 30 long minutes, the shoreline again loomed grey and surreal, and out of the gloom emerged another vehicle. Well, actually the same one – mine – again. The sole saving grace: no witnesses, save Belle with her puzzled look.

Before Belle, our family had a great dog named Keesh. He was a proud protector of our girls, was incredibly faithful to all of us and loved any kind of adventure. But he wasn't perfect. One of his faults, perpetuated by the inadequate training he'd received from me, was that he tended to venture too far ahead when we were hunting ring-necked pheasants. When that happened, he would flush roosters well out of gun range. My quick fix: a 20-metre check cord linking us together.

One crisp autumn morning, Keesh and I were hunting among low willows lining a steep riverbank where the water had frozen along the edges. Suddenly a cackling rooster flushed five metres away. Feeling rather sporting, I let him fly out a bit before shooting. He was halfway across the river when I fired my second barrel, which was just as ineffective as the first. Unmarked, the rooster flew to the far bank, where he landed and vanished in the willows.

I was still cursing my marksmanship when – with the slow-mo horror of a car crash happening before your eyes – I realized that Keesh was still running full tilt toward the river. He didn't know the bird had escaped. Problem was, the check cord was still attached to my waist. Suddenly everything changed to fast motion. When Keesh hit the end of the rope, which coincided with his reaching a third of the way across the river, I felt a mighty, jolting tug. Pulled off balance, I launched like a missile off the mud-slicked bank. Luckily, I had just enough time to toss my empty shotgun into the willows. Upon landing in the river, I crashed through the ice – on my back.

After about 30 seconds of over-theatrical splashing to regain my feet, I spat out muddy water while clambering out of the river and up the bank, where I stood shivering. Fortunately, I still had the presence of mind to have a quick look around. Much to my relief, again there was no mob of onlookers. On the other hand, I swear that Keesh wasn't merely smiling but seemed to be laughing uproariously.

All hunters have had experiences they'd rather forget, or wish hadn't happened – even though they have nothing to do with ethics. Combined with all the other ingredients of the hunt, these mishaps are invariably woven into the colourful fabric of the overall experience. They give us stories to tell around the campfire, and they inject some levity into an activity many of us sometimes take far too seriously.

But if you hunt alone, nobody ever has to know about these encounters of the red-faced kind. Unless, that is, you choose to spill the beans.

ON THE WATER

A RIVER RUNS
THROUGH ME

*Eventually, all things merge into one, and a river
runs through it. The river was cut by the world's
great flood and runs over rocks from the basement
of time. On some of the rocks are timeless raindrops.
Under the rocks are the words, and some of the
words are theirs. I am haunted by waters.*

Norman Maclean,
A River Runs Through It

On a bookshelf in my home office, under a framed original
Jack Cowin line drawing of a brown trout, sit two vintage
brass fly-fishing reels, a three-inch-square glass paper-
weight with a rainbow-hued Garry salmon fly imbedded
in it, and an empty, slightly tacky tin that once contained
a sugary confection called Trout Tin Fisher-Mints. "Don't
get caught with fish breath!" admonishes the script-type
lettering on the tin.

But these items are merely the supporting cast. They
aren't the most important things on the shelf.

That honour belongs to an seven-inch-long flat oval rock

that has been rubbed smooth by years, perhaps centuries, of being washed by running water, either a river or creek. It appears to have come *from the basement of time.*

On this rock, my wife, Karen, has lovingly and meticulously reproduced, in fine calligraphy printed with black marker, the touching passage that crowns this story, like rich ice cream atop a plain tasteless cone.

Iowa-born writer Norman Maclean wrote those mantric words in his famous novella *A River Runs Through It*, published in 1976. That was 16 years before Robert Redford turned it into an iconic movie starring Brad Pitt. The movie changed the popular view of fly-fishing. What had once been seen as a hobby for tweed-wearing elitist sportsmen was now recognized as a life-defining activity pursued by preachers, university students and, yes, even gambling newspapermen with a thirst for good bourbon.

Suddenly, everyone wanted to learn to fly-fish just like Brad Pitt, to inject some balance into their hectic lives, and in the process perhaps slow down life's roller coaster to a more manageable pace. They wanted fly-fishing to help them find a better place, either physically or metaphorically.

I'd been fly-fishing for many years when *A River Runs Through It* hit the silver screen. I was already one of the so-called converted. But the movie, and then the book (I saw it before I read it), helped open my eyes to how others see the activity that had become my passion, and the people who pursue it. Suddenly, fly-fishing took on a near-mystical quality for me.

Anyone who has ever fly-fished for any duration knows that it involves a lot more than just catching fish.

Oh sure, we catch fish, sometimes lots of fish, sometimes big fish and sometimes little fish. But there also are times when we don't catch any fish.

That's okay too.

It's okay because we're out in special places, beautiful places, usually away from crowds of people and always away from our desks, our volunteer and work obligations, the everyday pressures – factors that help define who we are but which can control or even overwhelm our lives if we let them.

It's okay because we're meeting the fish in their natural element, not ours. We are feeling the strong, surging current rush against our bodies, challenging us to stay upright, refreshing us, infusing us with energy and life itself.

It's okay because we are hoping to unlock the secret of the water that day, to find out what insect the trout are taking and to try to match that bug with the imitations in our fly boxes. It's part science, part crapshoot, a combination of gut feeling, experience and educated guess.

It's okay because the line feels cool and smooth as it runs through our fingers, the thin, plastic-coated thread the only physical connection between us, the water and, if we're lucky, the fish. The mere act of casting is tonic for the soul.

It's okay because we're watching dainty slate-grey American dippers flit from rock to rock, occasionally diving into the water in search of an insect.

But when the magic happens, when a fish actually takes our offered fly, it all comes together, initially making us feel delighted surprise, then excitement followed by anxiety that the fish might get away before we're ready. If it does slip the hook, we enter a fantasy world of speculation and exaggeration.

And when we finally gently slip our hands around the body of the fish – trout, salmon or other – we feel joy and, inexplicably, sometimes even sadness because that is yet another experience we've had, and we're not sure how many more we've been allotted.

That fish – every fish – becomes preserved in our memory banks, there to withdraw whenever our spiritual beings are in need of a lift.

Fly-fishers come to view rivers as living, breathing entities. We become like the rocks on the river bottom, the whispering words, the river's story.

When I'm fishing a river or stream, I find myself feeling envy of its freedom, its natural rhythm, how it moves and how it constantly finds a different way to go when confronted with boulders, logs and other constrictions. A river's structure is its character. It's what makes it strong.

I'm reminded of the words of Celtic poet John O'Donohue, who wrote:

I would love to live
Like a river flows,
Carried by the surprise
Of its own unfolding.

While on the water, we become part of rivers, their riffles, rapids, long and mysteriously deep reaches, quiet pools and side channels. We share them with the birds, animals and fish that live there, and sometimes even feel their often chilly lifeblood when we take a dunking, on purpose or by accident.

We know their promise. We sometimes become discouraged that we can't unlock their secrets. We remember when we have caught fish but also remember when a fish has beaten us at our own game.

We resent ourselves for doing bad things to rivers, and we try to be hopeful for their futures and for ours.

We become, as Norman Maclean so poetically described, haunted by them.

DREAM FISH

It happened during my childhood, half a century ago in Windsor, Ontario. Our family lived there from 1957 to 1960. All these years later, I still remember our address – 1510 Victoria – and I really remember the school principal strapping me for wolf-whistling at my gorgeous Grade 1 teacher.

But mainly, I remember *the fish*.

It was a Saturday morning, and Dad had taken me fishing along the Detroit River, which separates Windsor from Detroit. I would have been six or seven. To me, the river was huge. Even years later, after moving to southern Alberta, I remember thinking it made the Bow River look like a spring creek. After all, the shortest distance across the Detroit River is a half mile.

The day didn't exactly have an auspicious start. We were on a public walkway beside the river, where it flowed slowly and slightly brown several feet below us. On Dad's first cast with a heavy spoon, I watched wide-eyed as the lure flew through the air for what seemed like miles. When it finally splashed down, it was so far out I couldn't see it.

"Wow," I said. "You almost hit the other side."

But when I looked at my dad, I could tell something was wrong. He was staring with disgust at his empty reel. Seems he'd recently added some line, but had forgotten to connect the end of the line to the spool. He'd just cast out the entire length, losing his favourite spoon in the process. He quickly re-spooled and resumed fishing.

Frankly, I don't remember doing much fishing myself. I was just there to share a rare day with Dad. I spent most of my time doing what kids do: watching gulls and passing boats, and hoping against hope that my father would catch a big one. But the fish wouldn't cooperate.

At one point, bored spitless, I peered into the water from over the edge of the walkway. All I saw was dirty foam, paper, scraps of wood, the odd empty bottle and other bits of trash. But then there was something else, a very large something else – cruising from right to left was the biggest fish I'd ever seen. Heck, I thought it was the biggest fish in the world. It was just a few feet under the murky water, and all I could see was its featureless shadow, which looked to be at least eight feet long.

My pulse racing, I called Dad over to see it. "Is it a shark?" I asked.

"There aren't any sharks here," he replied, then resumed fishing, as if this sort of thing happened every day.

For the rest of that day on the walkway, I kept my eyes glued to the water, hoping the giant fish would return so we could hook him. It didn't, and I never saw it again on later trips to the river. Heck, I've never seen a fish like it since.

Most anglers have experienced one such fish, and those

who haven't surely dream about it, a specimen so fantastic in every way that it almost reaches the status of legend. Except it isn't a legend, because legend suggests fiction, and there's nothing fictional about such a fish. It is very real when it comes into your life, and it remains so until you make your last cast.

It could be a huge fish you never landed, on the line just long enough for your adrenaline to surge and your heart to race. Or maybe, like the giant fish of my childhood, you only saw it, cruising in the shallows, or perhaps rising to a fly, chasing a lure or leaping out of the water for no other apparent reason than to tease.

Norman Maclean wrote that he was haunted by waters. Me too, but I'm also haunted by the vision of that giant fish, which, many years later, I've decided must have been a sturgeon. It has stayed with me all this time, imprinted on my psyche, remembered always as *the one*.

My fish of a lifetime.

THE OPENER

Opening Day.

Trout fishers dream of it, plan for it and relish it with the excitement of a child at Christmas. It means winter is finally over, spring has returned like a long-lost friend and the trout are waiting.

There is the promise of big trout, lots of them. Forgotten are the frustrations of seasons past, of the trout that got away courtesy of a weak leader or dull hook. Still locked in our memories are the trout of years past that were hooked, fought, landed and perhaps released to propagate the species. We remember every one.

Spring is a time of renewal for streams and rivers, which have sung their siren songs to anglers for centuries. Snow is melting, on some days swelling flowing waters with murky runoff. Rainbow and cutthroat trout are using their tails like shovels, digging redds in gravel riverbeds, creating pockets where they can lay and fertilize their eggs. The trout are driven by an irrepressible instinct to give new life for their species and, as a side effect, hope for anglers now and in the future.

In *The Year of the Trout*, author Steve Raymond writes:

Spring brings
fulfillment
of an angler's winter dream;

A chance again
to solve
the silent silver secrets of the stream.

How true.

Spring also brings renewal to the land through which waters flow. Velvety pussy willows sprout on bushes, while forests and grasses start turning green and lush. Plumage on male birds is resplendent with brilliant colour, all the better to turn the eye of a potential mate. Female deer and elk heavy with fawn and calf vanish into birthing areas; opportunistic cougars, coyotes, wolves and bears follow them.

Mornings are fresh and cool, the dew still heavy on the ground many hours after dawn. Days are short; those marathon trout-fishing sessions extending well past dark remain a distant probability, not a present reality.

Even in regions where anglers can fish legally for trout in flowing waters through the winter, springtime holds a special allure. Fishing open water in winter is only a stopgap, a bonus season and an excuse to fish without having to use an auger. Banks are icy and treacherous, water crowded with ice floes. Winter trout are lazy, often needing a lure or fly bounced off their nose to entice them to strike.

Spring trout are a different story. They are hungry, brightly coloured and increasingly active as the world around them comes to life. They emerge from the obscurity of winter, venture out of deep mysterious holes and scatter to holding stations where they wait for food, or claim a breeding territory. They show themselves more readily, chasing each other off their redds or breaking the surface to claim a passing meal. Put simply, spring trout are more aggressive, which means they are much more likely to nail a spinner, bait or fly. For the angler, that is good news.

Spring is a season of promise and hope. It means streams and rivers are slipping off their icy cloaks, opening up the wonderful world of the most popular and exciting resident trout species: eastern brook, rainbow, brown, cutthroat and bull.

Now is the time to don waders and ease into the chilly water, to return to that comfortable state of being, like those childhood visits to your grandmother's house. It is a time to stretch those winter-weary muscles, reignite that passion for the chase, oil that reel, replace last year's line, fix that dangling ferrule, tighten the drift boat's loose oarlock and sort the tackle box or fishing vest.

Springtime on the water is a time for making lifelong memories.

Like the spring a couple of years ago, when my youngest teenaged daughter, Sarah, and I headed to a favourite southern Alberta river famous for its rainbows, browns, bull trout and an increasing population of frisky cutthroats.

That day, we watched an American dipper, a slate-coloured bird, dive for insects in the newly ice-free water, then return to the surface to stand on a rock, bobbing its head continually like a punch-drunk boxer.

Later, we stood in silence as a mule deer doe picked her way through the willows on the other side of the river. Several times, we stopped our bankside meandering to spy on big rainbow trout as they chased interlopers from their redds. Oh yeah, we caught and released a few trout that day; nothing huge, but enough to add icing to an already great outing.

A few springs before, I'd visited the same river with Sarah's older sister, Chelsea. We ended the day fishing a gorgeous deep pool where the river takes a bend to the east. The locals call it the Family Pool. After wading out several feet, Chelsea began casting a San Juan Worm nymph weighted with several split shots.

For 30 minutes, nothing happened. Then her orange strike indicator suddenly vanished beneath the surface, and Chelsea was onto a good fish. A few minutes later, she briefly cradled a 20-inch bull trout in her hands before gently slipping it back into the water. We watched it swim away. "I can't believe I caught that fish," Chelsea said, her voice filled with awe and excitement.

I could believe it. When you are spring trout fishing, anything can happen.

And it often does.

RODERICK'S AMAZING
VANISHING ROD

Imagine accidentally breaking a hockey stick Wayne Gretzky lends you, or trashing a tennis racquet that Serena Williams lets you use. Even worse, how about watching helplessly as the tip section of a Roderick Haig-Brown fly rod you've borrowed from his daughter sinks into an icy mountain lake?

I still shudder at the memory.

Haig-Brown came into my life shortly after his 1976 death, when Karen gave me a copy of his 24th book, *Bright Waters, Bright Fish*. It hooked me on both fly-fishing and conservation writing. I became a Haig-Brown disciple. In this book and his many others, he expounds against hydro dams, logging, mining and poor attitudes that threaten fish and fishing. With equal fervour, he celebrates the joy of angling.

It's hard for anyone, but especially for an avid fly-fisher and conservationist, to not be totally enthralled by Haig-Brown's writing. In his 1946 book *A River Never Sleeps*, the author took many pages to eloquently address the question "Why fish?"

I still don't know why I fish or why other men
fish, except that we like it and it makes us think
and feel. But I do know that if it were not for the
strong, quick life of rivers, for their sparkle in the
sunshine, for the cold grayness of them under
rain and the feel of them about my legs as I set
my feet hard down on rocks or sand or gravel, I
should fish less often ...

Perhaps fishing is, for me, only an excuse to be
near rivers. If so, I'm glad I thought of it.

Haig-Brown's words ring so true to me.

Over the next several years, as my Haig-Brown book
collection grew, so did my devotion and respect. I fished
alongside him, in spirit, in his beloved Campbell River and
in more exotic waters around the world. Philosophically,
we were on the same page. I found myself often nodding
in agreement at quotations like this: "There will be days
when the fishing is better than one's most optimistic fore-
cast, others when it is far worse. Either is a gain over just
staying home."

Fast-forward 20 autumns to an international nature
writers' workshop in Waterton Lakes National Park in
southwestern Alberta. Valerie Haig-Brown, Roderick's
eldest daughter and a highly accomplished writer and editor, is an organizer. After some arm-twisting on her part,
I "volunteer" to co-lead a fly-fishing expedition along a

five-kilometre uphill trail leading to a spectacular alpine lake.

At the trailhead, I'm delighted to discover Valerie is among the participants. She greets me with a smile and an offer I can't refuse.

"I brought something for you to use," she says. "One of my dad's old rods."

At that, Valerie pulls out a short navy-blue cotton bag with white ties. My heart reacts like a Geiger counter at Chernobyl. I'm going to use *Roderick Haig-Brown's fly rod!*

The bag's label says "Hardy" in large letters. Valerie opens it and withdraws a four-piece eight-foot fibreglass six-weight rod marked with the name "Smuggler" on the butt section.

"My dad called this his suitcase rod," Valerie tells me. "He bought it for a trip to Italy but died before he could take it."

I'm so euphoric I virtually float along the trail during the two-hour hike. Finally reaching the lake, we encounter temperatures hovering around freezing and a mix of rain, sleet and snow. But I don't care. I'm going to fish with Roderick Haig-Brown's rod!

Reverently, I carefully string the rod and affix a reel. I imagine Haig-Brown cradling it a quarter century earlier. I tie on a green woolly bugger streamer weighted with a tungsten beadhead, then venture out onto a rocky outcrop to start casting.

My technique is simple. Let the fly sink to a count of three, and then retrieve it slowly. On the tenth cast, a feisty rainbow trout strikes. The 15-inch fish is quickly landed and released. When it's followed by two more within the next hour, I tell myself it's the Haig-Brown magic. I begin to feel a little cocky, like there's nothing to this.

Then, disaster.

After casting out the woolly bugger, I hesitate too long before starting the retrieve. The heavy fly plunges to the bottom of the lake and snags in the rocks. When I tentatively apply light pressure on the line, I can feel the fly is solidly stuck. As if that's not bad enough, when I wiggle the rod to try to free it, the tip section suddenly detaches from the other half of the rod, then slides down the line and, in nightmare-like slow motion, vanishes in the icy dark-blue depths.

For several horrifyingly long minutes, I stand frozen, fearing I'll break the line and doom the rod tip to the lake bottom. I gently give a few light tugs. Still stuck.

I move around to try different angles. No luck.

Despite the cold, I am sweating profusely and my hands start nervously shaking. I am absolutely certain I'm going to lose this rod tip. How would I explain that to Valerie? Thankfully she and the other hikers are tucked into a rocky shelter further down the shoreline and can't see my dilemma. Hoping against hope and in sheer desperation, I give the line one last little tug.

The fly comes free!

My nerves taut as a guitar string, I retrieve the line, relaxing only when the drowned tip section comes into view and clears the water. The streamer's large hook is all that's saving it from a watery grave, and me from eternal disgrace.

With a quick glance to ensure nobody's looking, I reattach the tip section, more firmly this time. This dream fishing trip is over. I've caught three beautiful trout on Roderick Haig-Brown's rod. And I didn't lose it. What more could I ask for?

I hike back along the lakeshore to meet the others.

"How was it?" Valerie asks upon seeing me.

I freeze in panic. What can I say? What should I say? That I almost lost her famous dad's rod? That it was pure luck that I didn't?

There is only one thing I can say to Valerie. The truth, minus a few incriminating details.

"It was just wonderful," I reply, with as much calm as I can muster.

"This rod is magical."

AFTER THE GOLD RUSH

George Bahm eased the aluminum boat into a peaceful bay and cut the motor.

With dusk fast approaching night, he strung an eight-weight graphite fly rod, tied on a cigar-sized white-and-red streamer, and suggested I do the same. Bahm scanned the water, searching for a sign – flash of panicked baitfish, torpedo-like wake of a large fish below the surface – anything that would indicate the presence of lake trout feeding in the shallows. But all we saw were scattered dimples of smaller fish rising for insects.

"Grayling," observed the seasoned Yukon guide. "But let's go for lakers. This is a great spot."

Frankly, I was beyond caring. I was just happy to be there, fulfilling a lifelong dream of fishing in the Yukon, Canada's northwesternmost territory, where moose far outnumber the human population of 32,000.

After I prepared my own eight-weight, George and I started casting. Time and again we threw floating lines and stripped back the Deceivers in our quest for a lunker laker. Nada. No strikes. Not even any trout cruising beneath the boat.

Eventually, I had a revelation. Here I was trying to catch lake trout that didn't seem to be here, while dozens of wild

Arctic grayling – a species I'd caught only in stocked lakes in southwestern Alberta – were rising within easy casting range.

I promptly rigged a four-weight and tied on a No. 16 Parachute Adams dry fly, then cast where a grayling had just risen. The fly sat unmolested maybe three seconds. Then a grayling had it. Several heart-pounding seconds later, I gently held a handsome male fish and admired its prominent iridescent dorsal fin before releasing it. Then I caught six more grayling in six casts.

"You must like catching those little fish," deadpanned Bahm.

"I'd rather catch grayling on a dry fly than nothing on a streamer, like some of us are doing," I replied.

Bahm kept casting his streamer, not frantically but with measured intent, looking very much like a guy who had already caught more fish in 36 years than most people would in ten lifetimes.

Bahm is a child of the Yukon wilderness. His mother, Doris, is a member of the Teslin Tlingit First Nation in southeastern Yukon, and his late father, Pius, was German. Born in the capital city of Whitehorse, George was raised with Native traditions and grew up in the bush – trapping, fishing and hunting moose and caribou.

But the lure of open skies proved irresistible. Bahm earned his wings when he was 18 and works as a pilot for Alkan Air, flying charters and emergency medevac missions to remote – heck, it's all remote – corners of the Yukon. When he's not flying, Bahm guides anglers, teaches fly-casting or fly-fishes by himself. "Fly-fishing keeps me real," he says.

The licence plate on his truck reads 2FLY, a nod to his dual passions of flying and fly-fishing. Co-workers, store clerks and friends regularly address him as "2FLY" instead of his real name.

Bahm's family owns a log cabin beside a creek overlooked by the Big Salmon mountain range in Yukon's south end. George uses the cabin as a four-season retreat and as a base for the annual moose hunt with his mother. His Teslin Tlingit grandfather is buried nearby in a sacred site.

As we fished until eleven p.m. on that calm August night, Bahm pointed to the nearby shoreline, where he caught his first fish – a grayling – more than three decades ago.

When it finally got so dark we couldn't see our flies, Bahm steered the boat back up the lake. Supper awaited in the cabin, a 90-minute truck ride away. The cold spray from the wake splashed my face as I sat motionless, staring in awe at the surrounding mountains silhouetted against the night sky. Occasionally, I had to pinch myself to prove I wasn't dreaming.

★ ★ ★

Getting to the Yukon took me almost 50 years. Although I've spent time in northern Manitoba, Saskatchewan and Alberta, the Yukon had seemed an elusive dream destination. I'd read about the Gold Rush, and as a kid had devoured Jack London's *The Call of the Wild* and *White*

Fang. I knew about Yukon's legendary fishing – for lake trout, grayling, northern pike, trout, salmon and inconnu – but didn't get to experience it for myself until summer 2002.

A day after landing in Whitehorse, which holds more than two-thirds of the people in this territory of 484,450 square kilometres, I headed west on the Alaska Highway toward Haines Junction. The scenery simply overwhelms – miles and miles of unspoiled wilderness, trees, mountains, glaciers and blazing patches of magenta-coloured fireweed, Yukon's official flower.

It was wonderful, but it was my second day in the Yukon and I still hadn't fished.

That was remedied a few hours later, when I arrived at Dalton Trail Lodge, just outside the eastern boundary of Kluane National Park. This luxurious yet rustic resort sits on the shore of 16-kilometre-long Dezadeash Lake, home to lake trout, grayling, pike, whitefish and burbot.

Eager to cast my first Yukon fly before supper, I grabbed my rod, vest and waders and followed owner Hardy Ruf's directions to the mouth of a nearby feeder stream. I was surprised to find two spin-fishers already fishing the creek. My heart really started to thump as I watched them catch and release grayling after grayling, all 6 to 14 inches long and all taken on small spinners.

By this time, it was late afternoon and grayling were rising to feed on the surface all along the creek. My nerves couldn't take it any longer. I had to fish now.

Hands shaking and mind preoccupied with rising grayling, I somehow managed to snap off the leader while uncoiling fly line from the reel. I discovered it's virtually impossible to tie an otherwise simple nail knot to link the two ends while standing mere feet away from your first Yukon grayling.

Finally, after several attempts, I completed the knot and tied on a tiny dry fly. The cast wasn't pretty, but it worked. A grayling sipped the fly and the four-weight bent double. Over the next 90 minutes, I caught and released dozens of grayling – all on dry flies. The Yukon was living up to its reputation, and then some.

The next day dawned cool, damp and overcast. From the lodge, I noticed fresh snow dusting the tops of rocky peaks in the Saint Elias Range in Kluane National Park. I winced, knowing that guide Doug Thomas and I planned to fish in the park that day. Thomas, who has guided in the Yukon for 27 of his 58 years, remained confident.

After breakfast, we hopped into a four-wheel-drive vehicle to travel to Mush Lake, accessible via a 22-kilometre dirt trail. En route, Thomas regaled me with tales of fly-fishing for big lake trout. We drove through spectacular scenery – distant mountains, valleys, forests and open meadows pitted with beaver ponds dimpled with rising fish. Although I'd hoped to see a Kluane grizzly bear – at a safe distance – our wildlife viewing was limited to a few ducks.

After loading our gear into a boat, Thomas and I motored

across the lake to the mouth of a river, where he'd enjoyed great action just a few days before. But snowmelt and rain from the night before had dirtied the river, creating a silty plume in the lake around the mouth. We spent an unproductive hour standing chest-deep in water, casting large streamers to lakers that either weren't there or just weren't feeding.

Fishing picked up, however, when we moved to a river connecting Mush with another lake. Bear spray in hand, Thomas and I hiked a few hundred metres from the lake into a set of waterfalls tumbling into calmer, clear water. Grayling seemed to be rising everywhere. Sometimes their entire bodies cleared the water, huge dorsal fins slicing the surface when they dove back in.

We caught dozens of fish on dry flies, from Black Gnats to Humpies and Parachute Adams to Elk Hair Caddis. The fishing was just as good as I'd had the day before; the difference was that these fish were several inches larger, with some approaching 18 inches and three pounds. Hooking a grayling like that on a light fly rod is an incomparable thrill.

On the way back to the vehicle, Thomas pulled the boat into a calm bay where he'd caught lake trout before. Even casting with a large spoon failed to produce. Lake trout, it seemed, just weren't to be. It was to be a harbinger for my laker outing with George Bahm the next day.

As it turned out, I didn't encounter lake trout until my last two days in the Yukon.

Fishing out of the remote Tagish Wilderness Lodge on Tagish Lake, straddling the Yukon–British Columbia border, owner Beat Korner and I caught plenty of lake trout while deep-trolling with heavy tackle using spoons, cisco baits and downriggers. We both had fish on that we couldn't budge off the bottom, but the biggest laker we landed was about six pounds.

I certainly wasn't complaining – especially when I got to stay in a cozy log cabin that Beat and his wife, Jacquie, had named Jack London. Occasional howling from their kennel of 23 sled dogs underscored the wilderness experience.

★ ★ ★

It's possible that George "2FLY" Bahm's propensity for fishing where lakes and rivers join is rooted in his Teslin Tlingit heritage. After all, *Teslin* in the Tlingit language means "mouth of the river," while *Tlingit* itself means "people." Or it might be that Bahm just knows from experience that river mouths are grayling hot spots.

Whatever the explanation, I certainly wasn't complaining as we started our second day of fishing together. Under a light rain, we boated past the bay where we'd fished the night before. As we entered the fast-moving, shallow river, Bahm suggested I tie on a weighted nymph pattern. A few seconds later, I flipped out a beadhead Prince nymph below a small foam indicator. A grayling immediately rose and hit the indicator, which was then pulled under by another fish that took the nymph below it. I lifted the rod tip and was fast onto a 17-inch grayling, the first of more than 20 I would land in the next half-hour.

We proceeded further down the river, stopping occasionally to wade the better water. By now I'd switched to a dry fly, and the fishing never slowed. On a bend in the river, we found dozens of big grayling – four-pounders pushing 20 inches – rising to a hatch of mayflies. As rain fell and we caught fish after fish, it dawned on me that this was the best fishing I'd ever enjoyed. At one point, I stopped fishing to watch Bahm make a perfect cast and hook another fish. Suddenly, I spied movement beyond him on the other side of the river.

A black bear sow and her new cub were crawling over a tangle of tree roots, completely oblivious – or perhaps not caring – that we were just 70 metres away. They disappeared in the trees without once acknowledging our presence. We later saw an osprey, a bald eagle and a chocolate-brown mink scurrying along the shore.

Later that afternoon, the rain and wind picked up and the fishing slowed. Bahm selected a spot for lunch on a gravel point and busied himself preparing food while I collected firewood. When I returned, my arms were laden with deadfall. Bahm pointed at my heavy load and laughed.

"An Indian makes a small fire and sits close," he said, smiling. "A white man makes a big fire and keeps warm by collecting wood."

So we made a medium-sized fire and called it a day. A very good day in an amazing place.

CHASING CATS

Catfish were considered garbage fish when I was growing up in Winnipeg. Whenever we accidentally caught one of these ugly, whiskered creatures while fishing for more desirable species such as walleye, we'd disdainfully throw it back in the water, always accompanied by considerable ribbing from our fishing partners.

So what was I doing, many decades later, in a boat on the Red River, fishing with a professional guide for the sole purpose of catching a giant catfish?

Having lots of fun, that's what.

"Get ready for a fishing adventure like you've never had before," guide Todd Longley announced when we met at the pier in the town of Selkirk, just north of Winnipeg, shortly after sunrise one Friday last June.

Typical hype, I remember thinking.

How wrong I was.

Forty-five minutes later, the tip of the heavy fibreglass rod started an almost imperceptible *tap-tap* motion, signalling a biting fish. I instantly moved toward the rod tucked in the holder affixed to the gunwale, but Longley cautioned me to be patient.

"Give it time to really eat the bait," he said.

A few seconds later, he shouted, "Now!"

With that, I cranked back on the rod and felt nothing but dead weight. I thought I was snagged on the bottom – until the "snag" started moving and pulling back.

Although the fish fought hard, it was no match for the 30-pound test line and sturdy rod. After a few minutes, Longley netted the channel catfish and handed it to me. At 32 inches long and 14 pounds, it was the biggest freshwater fish I'd ever caught.

"That's just a baby," Longley noted, smirking.

He should know. Since he started his City Cats guiding service in 1999, Longley has guided clients from across North America to thousands of huge channel catfish up to 37 pounds.

Longley strives to put his clients into Manitoba's Master Angler (MA) awards record book, which requires anglers to catch a fish of a specified minimum length, with witnesses to prevent cheating. For channel catfish, that number is 34 inches. (A 46.5-inch monster caught in 1992 is Manitoba's biggest recorded catfish).

Even though I'd fished in Manitoba since I was a kid, I'd never caught a fish of any species that qualified for a MA award.

Longley had vowed to correct that. So had my fishing partner for the day, Shel Zolkewich, a freelance writer who works as the fishing and hunting consultant for Travel Manitoba. When Zolkewich issued the invitation to fish for catfish, she also promised to out-fish me. Her exact words – "I'm going to kick your butt" – were a little daunting.

So was the guide. Longley, 47, bills himself as the Rock and Roll Fisherman. Even though he's never played an instrument or sung a note on stage, he looks the part: husky build, straggly shoulder-length hair and scruffy salt-and-pepper beard. He was wearing a sleeveless Harley Davidson T-shirt, faded jeans and red-laced and red-soled running shoes. His chunky biceps sport tattoos, including a scary-looking catfish on his left arm. Longley's professional motto, "Go Big or Go Home," seems redundant when taken in this overall context.

After working the graveyard shift on the dock of a soft drink company in Winnipeg, Longley jumps in his truck to guide clients in his 19-foot fibreglass boat powered by a 150-horsepower motor. Many of those clients are eager to hook into big cats, which he calls "the alpha predator in the river."

Fishing for Manitoba catfish became popular about 20 years ago, when anglers began catching tackle-testing 20- to 30-pound fish in the Red River, which flows north from Minnesota and North Dakota through Winnipeg and into Lake Winnipeg. The Red River soon became known as the catfish capital of North America. It boasts 90 per cent of the catfish that qualified for Master Angler awards. They thrive on plentiful goldeye, sauger and other fish, and are protected by provincial regulations that require bigger fish to be released.

Word spread and soon anglers were visiting from Missouri, Nebraska and other states famous for catfish.

Although catfish can be excellent eating, almost all the cats caught in Manitoba are released. While anglers don't fish for them for the table, nor do they seek them for their good looks. Catfish are ugly. Their smooth bodies are blue-grey with white on the bottom. Their heads are huge, with wide toothless mouths fringed with whisker-like barbels equipped with sensors used to find food on muddy river bottoms.

"There's something slightly comical about catching a fish that's so ugly – in a loveable way," Zolkewich says.

Most anglers fish for them for one reason: to experience the brute strength of a big catfish at the end of the line.

In recent years, the catfish's unlikely star continued to rise through American reality television shows like *Hillbilly Handfishin'*, in which guests use their hands and feet to catch big cats in Oklahoma rivers and lakes. It's called "noodling."

Much to my wife's chagrin, I love that show. Chasing the big whiskered trash fish of my youth became a dream. But Winnipeg is closer than Oklahoma, and so I became determined to tackle a big catfish the more traditional way.

That's how I found myself on the Red River last June. After landing that first "baby" catfish, Zolkewich and I managed to catch a few freshwater drum, also called silver bass, including one that missed qualifying for a Master Angler award by just one-quarter of an inch.

We were using a popular technique. With the boat anchored in the sluggish yet powerful current, we fished hooked hunks of goldeye and jumbo-sized prawns held on the muddy bottom with a four-ounce lead weight. Catfish bite tentatively, causing the rod tip to dance lightly. Longley urged us not to set the hook until the fish begins to pull down on the rod steadily. It's a waiting game, but luckily the wait is never long.

As the morning heated up in the blazing sun, I hooked another cat. At 16 pounds, this one was bigger than the first but was just 33.5 inches long, missing the elusive Master Angler mark by a mere half-inch. Minutes later, another fish bit and I knew this was it.

The fish hugged the bottom for what seemed an eternity before I could budge it. After a lot of give and take, I managed to bring it to the waiting net. When Longley laid it along the official tape affixed to the boat seat, it measured exactly 34 inches. My first Master Angler fish. After the 20-pounder was released, I high-fived Longley and Zolkewich and declared that the next fish was hers.

My mistake. At noon, one of the rods in the holders started throbbing and Zolkewich grabbed it. The fish took her from one side of the boat to the other, but she wasn't giving up. Finally, Longley slipped the net under the fish and hoisted it aboard.

It was the biggest cat of the day, at 35.5 inches long and 25 pounds. Although Zolkewich already had "maybe two or three" MA awards for channel catfish, this was her biggest one ever.

More importantly, at least to her, it was bigger than mine.

"I told you I was going to kick your butt," she said. "How do you feel now?"

Ouch.

TROUT BUM

Being a trout bum has its moments, and this was one of them. John Gierach's bamboo fly rod was imitating an upside-down U, throbbing under the weight of a big Bow River brown trout he'd enticed from its watery lair under a willow bush hanging out over the water. "It feels like a good fish," said Gierach, who knows in his heart that every trout is a good trout, no matter how big.

Fighting the Bow's spring-runoff-swollen current, stocky ex-military guide Dave Brown laid into the oars of the McKenzie drift boat and steered toward the far shore. Gierach held on, grim-faced, as the trout came along none too willingly. After easing the 15-foot boat against the grass-lined bank, Brown hopped out and promptly netted the trout. A wide smile split the trout bum's grey-whiskered beard as he removed the streamer from the trout's lip.

Then he briefly held the yellowish, dark-spotted brown for the obligatory photograph before cradling it gently in the water. A few moments later, he silently watched the fish swim back into the murky depths.

Dave Brown pronounced it was 21 inches long.

"By the time I get home, it'll be 24," quipped Gierach. For

this trout bum, literary licence can be just as important as an angling licence.

Gierach is one of the world's best fly-fishing writers, distinguished by punchy, wit-seasoned stories, crisp writing, genuinely self-deprecating style – and a flair for, to put it politely, embellishment. He's the author of eight books, including popular cult classics *Trout Bum*, *Even Brook Trout Get the Blues* and *Sex, Death and Fly-Fishing*. A new book, *Dances with Trout*, is due out next year.

Gierach has been published in major outdoor magazines and writes columns for *The New York Times*, *Fly Rod and Reel* and the *Times-Call* of Longmont, near his wood-frame house on northern Colorado's St. Vrain River.

All this has brought unexpected favourable notoriety for the plain-talking, simple-living Gierach, who once worked as a garbage collector to pay the bills. It's also meant a comfortable lifestyle that allows him to fish in Scotland and other faraway lands – and write about it. Gierach concedes his success might appear to conflict with his projected image of a self-described trout bum living hand to mouth and hatch to hatch.

"I suppose a genuine trout bum wouldn't have a New York agent," says Gierach, 46, twice divorced and now resolutely single.

"But it's easier to be a trout bum with a little money than if you're broke. Fishing has kept me sane and made me a living."

Gierach had never even seen a trout before moving west to Colorado from Ohio in 1968. Since then, he's fly-fished for several trout species, bluegills, bass, northern pike and even long-nosed gar. His tip for gar: use a frayed rope instead of a hooked fly because the gar will tangle the rope around its toothy beak.

This week, after years of hearing about the venerable Bow River, Gierach finally had a chance to fish it. It clearly impressed him.

"Anytime you have a great trout stream like this flowing through a big city, you've got something to be really proud of," he says.

Brown invited me to be part of Gierach's initiation trip, early on a weekday morning on a stretch of river in the middle of Calgary. The trout weren't exactly cooperative; the murkiness of the water forced us to thrown big weighted streamers to try to draw trout from the depths instead of casting tiny, delicate dry flies for rising trout. At one point, fishing through a long, deep run with slabs of concrete lining the bank, I felt the solid take of a big, strong fish.

My heart raced as the fish took one long run after another. Gierach cast the odd casual glance my way, but all in all wasn't too interested as he continued to cast. Finally, the fish came close to the boat and Brown netted it. Instead of the huge brown trout I'd been hoping for, it was a 24-inch northern pike, the first I'd ever caught on the Bow. Although it's a decent fish, catching a pike on this world-famous trout fishery was like ordering a beer in a fancy wine bar. Gierach looked over with some disdain as I released it. "Nice pike," was all he said.

That morning, the Bow afforded Gierach his best brown trout of his trip – the 21- or 24-incher, depending on who you believed – along with a great one-liner. While floating a stretch of water through an industrial area, we passed underneath a tarp-covered railway bridge. The early-morning solitude was shattered by a power sandblaster working on the concrete overhead. It sounded like a massive dentist's drill as it showered us with sanded grit.

"I think I can honestly say that's the first time I've ever been sandblasted while fishing," Gierach said, smiling.

I could imagine the chapter heading already: "Getting Blasted on the Bow."

LESSONS THE TROUT TAUGHT ME

I was daydreaming about a rather unusual university. Fly rods and chest waders took the place of books and computers. Students joyfully waded the hallowed waters of great trout streams instead of glumly trudging along the hollow halls of academic learning.

The professors were huge brown and rainbow trout who eagerly taught their students the importance of humility and how little they knew about fly-fishing. The homework kept students on the water until all hours, and it seemed the lessons never ended.

But when I accidentally pinched myself with a pair of forceps while de-barbing an impossibly small fly, I discovered I wasn't dreaming after all. I actually was in Montana, a clueless freshman on the Missouri River, and I was failing Trout Fishing 101. Badly.

My enrolment at, let's call it, Missouri River University (or Miss U, for short) came about through a combination of fate and desperation. "Come to Montana this spring," urged my friend Mike, a dedicated repeat Missouri student. "My regular partner can't make it and I need someone to row."

My arm didn't need much twisting.

Everyone knows Montana is a fly-fishing mecca. Heck, it's the place Brad Pitt came to portray a gamblin', boozin' newspaper reporter in *A River Runs Through It*. The Madison, Big Horn, Jefferson, Flathead, Gallatin, Yellowstone – they're all legendary rivers that continue to beckon fly-fishers from around the world. But studying at Miss U held a special mystique.

I'd seen pictures and read articles about fly-fishing the Missouri, just five hours south of my home in southern Alberta. I'd driven past it many times, had even stopped on bridges to drool over the resident trout I could see swimming below me. But I'd never fished for them, even though I'd read many magazine articles and talked to friends about how great fly-fishing the Missouri can be.

Bruiser browns. Mighty rainbows. A fly-fishing paradise. Piece of cake, right? Well, so I thought, even though friends had warned me I should prepare to be educated by the Missouri. Stupidly, I had just scoffed at them.

★ ★ ★

Mike and I arrive late on a Sunday afternoon in mid-May, pulling into the tiny town of Craig (pop. 60, all fly-fishers, it seems), which some call the Fly-Fishing Capital of the United States. We're in time to buy angling licences and pitch our tent in the rustic campground beside the mighty Missouri. As we stand on the riverbank, nursing our beers, I begin seeing the river in a whole new light. It's a powerful piece of water, bigger and wider than the Bow back home, but with slower and flatter flows thanks to its tailwater status below Holter Dam. Montana author Trapper Badovinac likens it to "a spring creek on steroids."

At 4368 kilometres, the Missouri is the longest river in the US. For the next five days, Mike and I will walk-and-wade and drift my 12-foot aluminum rowboat along an 11-kilometre stretch between the Holter Dam and Craig. It's considered the best section in terms of trout numbers, insect life and accessibility.

I feel confident going into that first evening. I have a vestful of new flies, mainly midges and Parachute Adams and emergers, specially ordered as small as size 24. That's minuscule, about a third the size of the average wood tick. As we string our rods, Mike and I take turns standing on the high bank to admire dozens of huge rainbows and browns cruising in the clear water below.

Soon I'm waist-deep in the water on the other side of a small island, a few hundred yards upstream of Mike. The first trout rises five minutes later and my blood starts to boil. I can't tell what bug it came up for, but clearly it's a beauty. Fat, big-shouldered, tail like a spatula, at least 20 inches long, maybe 22. Fingers fumbling, I tie a size 22 Adams onto the end of a 12-foot leader tapered to a 5X (four-pound test) tippet. On the Bow back home, using a lighter tippet is considered foolhardy.

My heart skips a beat when the trout rises in the path my

fly is taking. The fly floats drag-free over the ring left by the surfacing trout, which duly ignores it for the first of many times. Soon several trout are rising regularly.

Three hours later, I haven't hooked a fish. I've switched fly patterns several times. But I continue casting, and the trout keep teaching me a lesson. It's my inaugural class at Miss U, and already I feel like a preschooler. When the sun finally drops behind the hills, I trudge back to the van. There sits Mike, shaking his head.

I'm secretly hoping that he has also scored a failing grade. "Did you hook any?" I ask.

"Stuck four or five and landed two," he replies. "You?"

"Zip."

We proceed to share war stories. I discover the secret of Mike's success. He started with 5x tippet. When that proved ineffective, he switched to 6x and then – incredibly – 7x. In case you're wondering, that's 3.6- and 2.7-pound test, respectively. He gently handled each hooked fish and lost those he rushed. "The trout reacted to 5x like it was rope," Mike notes. "It really spooked them."

No kidding, I thought.

That evening, we retire to one of Craig's two taverns. We sit at the bar, across from a grizzled, bearded cowboy who's obviously been here a while. Slumped over the bar, he looks up at us with bleary eyes and queries, "You boys fishing?"

When we nod yes, he sits up straight, his eyes narrow and he says one word: "Crawdads."

I'm hearing-challenged, so at first I think I heard him wrong.

"Crawdads?" I ask. "As in crayfish?"

"Yep. When nothing else works, when you've tried every fly you've got and you just can't catch one, tie on a crawdad. The trout love 'em."

Our mentor's words jump to mind the next day when I begin my morning class at Miss U. As I wade out into the river, I look down at the rocks and spot skeletal crayfish remains, perhaps left there by raccoons or river otters. I can't help but think: *I hope I never need to tie on a crawdad to catch a Missouri River trout.* To a committed fly-fisher, using a crawdad is akin to chucking dynamite.

I'll spare you the nasty details, but I don't catch a trout that day either. Not even a touch, even though I've tied on some new fluorocarbon 6x tippet. Throughout the day, I see many giant browns and rainbows, but they ignore everything I throw at them. But I do learn something important that day on the Missouri: not only are the fish smart, they also seem to be psychic. While eating lunch on the bank, Mike and I watch one big rainbow rise three times and decide to try for him. Before one of us can stand, though, the fish stops rising and swims away.

"All you have to do," Mike wryly observes, "is *think* about casting for these trout to put them down." Nonetheless, by day's end he has again earned top-of-the-class honours, landing several trout. My biggest thrill happens when a

24-inch rainbow chases a sculpin into an inch of water before gobbling it down, not three feet from where I stand, wide-eyed and envious.

★ ★ ★

In the campground the next morning, I encounter a portly good old boy in taut red suspenders. He's stringing a fly rod. "How're you boys making out?" he drawls in an accent oozing Southern US.

When I reply that my buddy is getting a few but I'm blanked, he nods, Yoda-like.

"These are the most educated trout in the country," he declares. "They've seen every fly there is to see and know how to avoid them."

As I walk away, I battle conflicting feelings. I'm happy because the Southern gentleman has confirmed that the problem isn't just me – these trout are really, really smart – but a little sad because I don't seem to be getting any smarter, which means I don't feel any closer to actually catching one.

Would I ever outsmart a Missouri River trout? I kept telling myself I will. The secret to fly-fishing is eternal optimism, leavened in the mantra that success isn't measured in numbers of fish landed. But still …

That morning I vow to change my attitude, to pay attention to my piscatorial professors and stop playing the class clown. I want to focus on my studies, not flog the water desperately. Relax, I tell myself. After all, I'm fishing some of the most gorgeous water I've ever visited and seeing more and larger trout than I ever thought possible, all amidst the spectacular beauty of central Montana's rolling hills, lush green carpets of spring grass and stunning pastel sunsets.

Mike and I decide to try a float. We head to the bridge at Wolf Creek, where a mini-flotilla of fancy pontoon and drift boats is putting in ahead of us. In contrast, my 12-foot aluminum craft is the nautical equivalent of a roped-together wooden raft. At least I can take some solace in the fact that it's the first boat that friend and fly-fishing guru Jim McLennan used for guiding on the Bow River 30 years ago. It's not a pretty craft, but it has history.

As we drift, we see countless trout darting about in the shallow, clear water below the boat. Although rising fish are few and far between, and common sense suggests nymphs, we are determined to stick with dry flies. We stop the boat several times, and Mike picks up a couple of nice rainbows. My fishless record remains intact.

Later that evening, still an hour away from the Craig bridge and with daylight fading fast, we beach the boat next to a long, flat stretch of water. A few trout rise periodically, taking tiny midges and the odd blue-winged olive mayfly. I cast a Griffith's Gnat and they promptly stop rising, completely uninterested.

Then another trout rises, and I cast almost absent-mindedly. It takes my fly. Setting the hook hard, I momentarily forget about the fragile 6x tippet. It snaps, and the fish is gone. Still, I am heartened; I've finally connected with a Missouri River trout, albeit briefly.

A few minutes later, I'm into another one. This time I set the hook with a gentle lifting of the five-weight rod. Line peels off the reel as the powerful trout surges for deeper water. When it stops running, I coax it back toward me. My heart beats furiously. The trout runs again and I let it. It stops just before hitting my backing.

Then the size 24 hook pops out. Just like that.

Disappointment floods through me. I look upstream and see Mike netting another big trout – his third of the night.

★ ★ ★

We decide to skip class at Miss U the next morning to fish a smaller local stream. The water is tea-coloured and the fish aren't feeding aggressively, but we (yes, me too) manage to land several hefty brown trout. Natch, Mike catches most of them, and while it's not the Missouri, at least I'm finally on the board.

Later, we stop to toast our success in a vintage small-town redneck bar. We stroll inside in our chest waders, the soaked felt soles leaving wet imprints on the carpet. The owner smiles as he snaps the bottle caps off a couple of Budweisers. Awaiting our fried chicken takeout, we admire hundreds of American dollar bills tacked on the walls and ceiling. On each one, people have written their names and hometowns. Some have even scrawled messages. "Bush sucks," one says. "Go &*%# yourself you liberal @#$%&*,"

shouts the one next to it. Even off the water, nothing in this part of the world is predictable.

That afternoon, Mike and I witness an angling approach new to us both – road fishing. As we cast unsuccessfully to trout on the east side of the Missouri, a truck hurtles down a gravel road flanking the river's far side. Two shirtless guys stand in the open box, scanning the water as they zip past. "Stop!" one of them suddenly shouts to the driver. "Look at those hawgs!" The truck skids to a halt in a cloud of dust. Fly rods in hand, the young men jump out and scamper down the bank. They cast several times, but nothing takes and they soon leave, road fishing for more trout.

★ ★ ★

It is cloudless and calm on our last morning, not ideal conditions for fly-fishing in clear, shallow water for possibly the smartest trout in North America. I still haven't landed a Missouri River trout and I'm feeling a little discouraged. It looks like I'll be finishing my first term at Miss U with a zero-point-zero grade point average. Mike and I assume our usual positions about 100 metres apart. Blue-winged olive mayflies are hatching and the fish are on them, with several trout rising at the outside range of my cast. Somehow I deliver a perfect cast and watch the Adams drift – miraculously and wonderfully drag-free – several feet. Suddenly a big rainbow sucks it in.

Fly line disappears in a flash, and the fish is soon into the backing, racing toward the middle of the river. Mindful of the 6x tippet, I carefully ease the trout back across the strong current. Then it takes off again, and I let it go. Confidence shattered by earlier encounters, I am sure I can't land this fish. Self-doubt nags at me, but I persist, reeling in the fish and letting it run two more times before it allows me to net it. My first Missouri River trout is a beautiful 22-inch rainbow. It took five days of frustrating cramming, but I feel like I finally aced an exam. The homework has paid off.

About ten minutes later, I spot a wide-shouldered brown repeatedly coming up to feed. My Adams slowly drifts downstream and I watch, amazed, as the trout surfaces to take the fly. It doesn't fight with the rainbow's vigor, but it gives it all it has – and then some. My backing is two revolutions of my reel away when the brown finally turns and comes to net. I scoop up the 20-incher and whoop with joy.

Two trout in one morning. Okay, two trout in five days. That might qualify as an F grade for most fly-fishers on the Missouri, but in my books it couldn't be sweeter. I've caught bigger trout, but never two that meant so much. To have it all happen on my last morning is incredible, well worth the price of enrolment.

Now I can go home knowing that although I didn't exactly graduate with honours from Miss U, at least I didn't flunk out miserably. Then again, a summer refresher course wouldn't be such a bad idea …

CONNECTING
THE DOTS

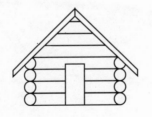

There are four buildings – three cottages and a log cabin. The cabin and one of the cottages are a few hundred kilometres apart in western Alberta. The second cottage is on Lake Winnipeg in Manitoba. The third is located deep in the Canadian Shield of northwestern Ontario. Despite the geographical separation, all four have been significant touchstones along my six-decade-and-counting adventure in the outdoors.

While growing up in Winnipeg, following brief stops in Windsor, Toronto, Calgary and Vancouver, I began fishing and hunting courtesy of my father, Bob. He taught my younger brother, Rick, and me to fish for yellow perch, white bass, walleye and northern pike off the pier at Victoria Beach on the southeast shore of Lake Winnipeg. Our family rented a cottage there for a few weeks each summer.

They were special summers, full of beach time, ice cream, hot dogs and fishing. The fishing was the best part.

Our technique was simple: a pickerel rig, a wire and monofilament contraption with a lead weight at the bottom and two bare hooks suspended above it. On those hooks we impaled salted minnows taken from a plastic margarine-style container. It seemed our fingers were constantly caked with minnow scales, and it was almost impossible to get rid of the fishy smell no matter how often we scrubbed with soap.

We sat on the pier, with our lines hanging down into the water below. When we caught a fish, it was reeled up the ten feet from the water to the pier. Then it was clipped onto a stringer attached to a rope and returned to the water until it was time to leave. At that point the fish were filleted and fried for supper.

We also regularly fished below the locks at Lockport, on the Red River north of Winnipeg. The three of us spent many hours standing on the shoreline, casting lures, spoons and salted minnows into the turbulent waters below the dam. We'd catch walleye, perch, white bass – all fine table fare – and the odd catfish, which we always threw back. One time Dad caught a ten-pound carp, a monstrous silver-scaled fish that he had to land by hand after his rod broke in mid-fight. We took it home and gave it to our Hebrew neighbours, who turned it into a traditional dish called Gefilte fish. It tasted awful.

When I was about 12, Dad and I started hunting for ruffed and spruce grouse in a provincial forest called Sandilands, about an hour east of Winnipeg. We would walk the trails for hours, shooting grouse with a .22 rifle or single-shot 12-gauge shotgun. All the birds were taken home and eaten. Within a few years I added snowshoe hares to my target species. Dad and I never hunted anything bigger; he had shot a deer when he was younger and didn't like the experience. I was 30 before I started hunting for deer, elk and moose.

Our fishing and hunting trips together were always fun, relaxing and special times, quite unlike our relationship at home.

My final happiest memory of Dad was when he was 80, two years before he died in a car accident. We fished together for yellow perch off a pier on the west shore of Lake Winnipeg. I drove us there, along with my younger brother. Dad was moving slower then, but he loved it. We baited Dad's hook and helped him land his fish, but he didn't care, because he was fishing. He'd done the same for us when we were kids.

While growing up, I became involved in Cubs and Scouts. Incredible volunteer leaders in those organizations mentored me in woodcraft, animal tracks, starting campfires, chopping wood, camping, hiking and snowshoeing. Although I love snowshoeing now, I hated it with a vengeance when I was a kid.

On weekends, my friends and I would pack a lunch and hike a few miles to a wooded area on the outskirts of Winnipeg, where we would spend all day building forts and lean-tos, setting cardboard box traps for rabbits (which always chewed through the cardboard and escaped), shooting arrows with our cheap bows and pretending we were deep in the wilderness.

But suddenly our family changed dramatically. Our

mother, Marybelle, died of cancer after a two-year struggle. She was 46. Just before the cancer diagnosis, she'd lost an eye to disease, so she had to cope with a prosthetic eye while in her dying days. Her death devastated Dad, my sisters Sue and Barb, 19 and 18 respectively, Rick, 12, and me, 15. We all dealt with it differently. My response was to direct extreme anger and bitterness at just about everyone, Dad especially.

When Mum's brother, Gary, drove from Alberta to the funeral in June, he took me back with him to spend the summer with his family, my Aunt Bett and three cousins. And there I stayed for almost two months, splitting our time between their home in Calgary and their new property at Crimson Lake in west-central Alberta.

They'd recently bought a lakefront lot and were starting to build a cottage on it. My job, ostensibly at least, was to help build it. Having never cut a board or even used a hammer much, I was more hindrance than help. On top of the lack of building skills, I was an emotional wreck most of the summer. When I was having my darkest days, Uncle Gary seemed to know I needed a break. Then he'd drive me to a nearby little creek, where I'd fish for several hours, alone in my grief but comforted by the peaceful setting and the few little trout I'd catch.

At Crimson Lake, which at the time was devoid of game fish, I was soothed by the beautiful yet eerie cry of loons, amazing sunsets and sunrises and, on one especially memorable morning, the sight of a massive cougar strolling past three feet in front of the screened-in porch. On days when we weren't building the cottage, we toured the remote countryside, fishing in streams and ponds and being awed by powerful waterfalls in surging rivers.

I was introduced to Banff National Park and other incredible areas I'd only dreamed about. The family treated me with kindness and generosity, and all seemed to sense when I needed to talk and when I wanted solitude. The cottage was almost finished by the time I returned home at the end of the summer.

Now, almost 50 years later, the cottage is gone but one of my cousins has built a four-season house on the site. Our family is welcomed there regularly, and we continue to enjoy the hiking trails, canoeing and kayaking, and the best sunsets and sunrises anywhere. The loons still call hauntingly, but now they share the lake with ospreys and blue herons, drawn by a healthy population of illegally introduced yellow perch. The perch have brought a pleasant benefit: we can finally fish in the lake itself, which often leads to tasty pan-fried perch fillets.

Crimson will always hold a special piece of my heart. That summer of 1968 had such an impact on me that after I returned to Winnipeg, all I could think about was someday returning to Alberta. Sure enough, when Karen and I were married in 1974 we moved west within two months. And here we remain.

The third cottage came into my life less than a year after my summer in Alberta. Dad remarried 11 months after Mum died. A widow whose first husband had also died of cancer, Margaret (we kids call her Marnie) made Dad very happy.

But in the myopia-inducing shock of seeing him married to another woman so soon after Mum's death, I found it challenging to welcome Marnie into our lives. One saving grace – very significant to a boy of 16 – was that she owned a cottage beside a remote lake called Malachi in northwestern Ontario.

The main access to Malachi was via a two-hour train ride on the CN main line from Winnipeg. For the next few summers, Dad, Marnie, Rick and I would ride the so-called Campers Special on most Friday evenings, munching fresh cinnamon buns and talking about what we were going to do at the lake that weekend. My little brother and I always hoped it would include fishing – and lots of it.

The cottage was a welcoming place. Marnie introduced us to her neighbours, who greeted us warmly, just like family. Rick and I revelled in the cottage experience: swimming, exploring the forest, chopping wood, helping with chores, catching crayfish in the rocks in front of the cottage, eating (Marnie seemed to be using vast quantities of delicious food to win us over) and, above all, fishing.

Often the four of us would head out together in a motorboat, angling for northern pike, walleye, yellow perch and smallmouth bass. Fish comprised many of our meals.

But the times I liked best were when Rick and I got to go fishing without Dad and Marnie. We weren't allowed to use the motorboat. Our assigned craft was a 14-foot heavy wooden rowboat that we called the Dory. It was equipped with a five-horsepower motor, which was barely enough to move it through the waves when the wind came up. But Rick and I didn't care, because we were fishing.

We were away from the happy newlyweds, by ourselves, free to go wherever on the lake we felt like going. We could talk openly about how much we missed Mum and about how much our new stepmother had changed Dad. We scanned the shoreline for moose and black bears. Loons and waterfowl bobbed on the waves. We cracked jokes and told stories. I'd escaped to Alberta the previous summer after Mum died, basically abandoning my little brother in his grief, and now it felt great to be reconnecting. I bonded with Rick in those summers at Malachi; my brother became my best friend.

All these years later, we still talk about the fishing, along with all our other Malachi memories.

The log cabin mentioned at the beginning of this story has had a more recent significant impact on my outdoor journey. Significant not because of the structure itself but because of the man who built it, log by log, chinking the walls and fitting the windows, so that he and his family could have a place to enjoy the land and the wildlife that lives on it.

Tom Beck is not a builder by trade. He's a hunter and

angler, and also happens to be one of Canada's unsung conservation leaders. And I'm proud to call him friend.

Tom was just 15 in 1947 when he and his mother emigrated to Canada from their home in Scotland. His father had died four years earlier. In Scotland, Tom regularly snuck into his neighbour's private woods, where he explored the natural world of hedgehogs, wild birds, bluebells and wild primrose flowers. A family friend used to take him fishing for trout and grayling in a nearby river, most of which was also privately owned.

For this outdoors lad, Alberta was just the ticket. Here, the outdoors are accessible to all, not just the wealthy. He discovered he could fish for trout in the Bow River and in remote streams, and soon took up hunting big game and game birds. Tom worked on improving his skills at viewing and identifying wild animals and birds, and developed a deep respect for the wild landscape.

That interest turned into a career working for resource companies in environmental affairs, especially in the Arctic, where he became one of the first industry people to advocate for involving northern Native people in government policies and industrial development. Tom then started an environmental consulting company and spent many years on the boards of provincial and federal conservation/environment organizations, including serving as commissioner of the federal land use planning commission for the Mackenzie Delta–Beaufort Sea.

Our paths crossed in the mid-1980s, when Tom was helping to broker the donation of 4,000 acres of private land as a conservation area just outside Calgary. At the time it was the largest donation of private land for conservation in Canada. I broke the story in the *Herald*, and years later Tom was instrumental in hiring me to write a book about it.

Our mutual interest in conservation led to a close friendship and many days together fly-fishing for trout and hunting for deer, elk, pheasants and waterfowl. The big-game hunting happens on a quarter section in the Wildcat Hills of Alberta's southern foothills. That's where Tom, now 84, built a beautiful rustic log cabin a few decades ago, followed by a second, smaller A-frame-style guest cabin.

I've stayed there many times over the years. It's high privilege to be invited, especially considering that one regular guest was his late good friend Ian McTaggart-Cowan, a world-renowned scientist and leader of environmental education and wildlife conservation in Canada. Ian and Tom hunted together for many years on his property.

Whether sitting in a tree stand or sharing a scotch at his kitchen table in the cabin he built, I've benefited greatly from Tom's wise and soft-spoken counsel – and also felt the brunt of his wicked Scottish sense of humour.

Although more than two decades separates us, Tom and I share a passion for the outdoors and a deep-rooted desire that future generations be able to enjoy it as we do.

There are four buildings – three cottages and a log cabin.

They provided shelter and a base for so many unforgettable outdoor experiences. But the people who occupied – and continue to occupy – those buildings gave those experiences context, richness and poignancy.

They made the memories worth keeping.

PREVIOUSLY PUBLISHED PIECES

SEASONS

Spring – *The Conservator*, Ducks Unlimited Canada (Spring 2002)

Summer – *The Conservator*, Ducks Unlimited Canada (Summer 2002)

Fall – *The Conservator*, Ducks Unlimited Canada (Fall 2002)

Winter – *The Conservator*, Ducks Unlimited Canada (Winter 2002)

NATURE

The Best Seat in the House – *A Hopeful Sign* blog (2013)

Stairway to Heaven – the book *Fly Like an Eagle: Real Life Stories of Hope and Inspiration* (2014)

The Not-So-Secret Place – *A Hopeful Sign* blog (2013)

Bird in the Hand – *Outdoor Canada* (Apr. 2004)

The Survivor – *Outdoor Canada* (Summer 2010)

Nature Makes Well – *Outdoor Canada* (Winter 2012)

Touching the Pine – Facebook post (Apr. 2016)

Night of the Wolves – reprinted with permission of *Calgary Herald* (Mar. 28, 1992)

KINSHIP

One Last Cast – reprinted with permission of *Calgary Herald* (Sept. 6, 1999); different versions of this story were published in *Reader's Digest* and the book *Chicken Soup for the Nature Lover's Soul*

The Creek – the book *From the Heart: Real Life Stories of Hope and Inspiration* (2015)

In Spirit – *Outdoor Canada* (Summer 2006)

Starting Them Young – the book *Inspiring Hope: One Story at a Time* (2013)

A Special Time and Place – a shorter version of this story was published in *Outdoor Canada* (Apr. 2002)

IN THE FIELD

A Natural Bond – reprinted with permission of *Calgary Herald* (Nov. 21, 1998)

Awakening the Senses – reprinted with permission of *Calgary Herald* (Oct. 11, 1999)

Passing the Buck – *Bugle*, Rocky Mountain Elk Foundation (May–June 2002)

Carl's Knife – reprinted with permission of *Calgary Herald* (Dec. 15, 1987)

Belle – *The Conservator*, Ducks Unlimited Canada (2009)

Hearing Voices – *Bugle*, Rocky Mountain Elk Foundation (May-June 2006)

The Embarrassing Truth – *Outdoor Canada* (Mar. 2001)

ON THE WATER

A River Runs Through Me – the book *Inspiring Hope: One Story at a Time* (2013)

Dream Fish – *Outdoor Canada* (Fishing Special 2010)

The Opener – *Outdoor Canada* (Apr. 2000)

Roderick's Amazing Vanishing Rod – *Outdoor Canada* (Apr. 2005)

After the Gold Rush – *Outdoor Canada* (Summer 2004)

Chasing Cats – *West* (Summer 2013)

Trout Bum – reprinted with permission of *Calgary Herald* (May 30, 1993)

Lessons the Trout Taught Me – *Outdoor Canada* (Apr. 2006)